Emigre No. 66

NUDGING
GRAPHIC DESIGN.

EMIGRE NO. 66

CO-PUBLISHED BY
PRINCETON ARCHITECTURAL PRESS
2004

Edited and designed by Rudy VanderLans.
Copy editing by Alice Polesky.

Emigre, 1700 Shattuck Ave., #307, Berkeley, California 94709
Visit our web site at www.emigre.com.

Co-published by Princeton Architectural Press
37 East Seventh Street
New York, New York 10003
For a free catalog of books, call 1.800.722.6657.
Visit our Web site at www.papress.com.

ISBN 1-56898-437-5
ISSN 1045-3717

CONTENTS

INTRODUCTION

IF YOU WANT TO KNOW what's on the minds of graphic designers these days, design blogs are the places to visit. I am completely hooked on reading at least one design blog every day. The first thing I do in the morning, after turning on my computer, is log on to Speak Up (underconsideration.com), a blog started in 2002 by Armin Vit (*see interview on page 17*).

Speak Up features a great variety of voices, from design students to designers who work strictly for non-profits, to those who work at some of the largest ad agencies in America. The discussions cover a rich spectrum of topics, ranging from in-depth talks on how to present your portfolio, to lengthy and heated debates on the redesign of the UPS logo.

Due to the variety of participants, the discussions regularly expose the uncomfortable fit between graphic design and advertising, and at times come to blows over such topics as the First Things First manifesto and the recent AIGA conference, which focused on sustainable design. But despite the differences of opinion, the point of view is strictly from within graphic design, and the topics are decidedly relevant to the practice of design — something most designers demand from any writing concerning design. In that respect Speak Up is by, for, and about graphic designers in the narrowest sense of the term. Consummate professionals that they are, it is also one of best designed and easiest to use blogs I have seen.

There are other design-related blogs I visit. Typographi.ca and Typophile.com are musts if you're interested in type design. If you think *Emigre's* discussions on legibility in the early 90s were somewhat tedious, check out the depth and extent to which these bloggers discuss the topic.

Another recent addition to the design blog universe is DesignObserver, run by William Drenttel, Jessica Helfand, Rick Poynor, and Michael Bierut. DesignObserver distinguishes itself from Speak Up by using a more serious tone and by casting a wider net. The creators' aim is to establish "a forum for a broader kind of critical writing on design issues." In a recent AIGA lecture, which sparked much discussion on Speak Up, Drenttel and Helfand restated the often heard complaint that "designers need to think and know more about things besides design" and show intellectual curiosity to foster cultural literacy, something they feel is lacking in design and design education. DesignObserver is their contribution towards that goal. Many of the topics on DesignObserver only touch tangentially on graphic design and are often inspired by articles published in the *Times Literary Supplement*, *The New Yorker*, and *The New York Times*. By taking ideas from the culture at large, they hope to expand their field of vision and discuss graphic design in new ways.

While passionate about design, DesignObserver's authors also question the kind of unconditional belief in the goodness of graphic design (and particularly design's role in advertising and branding) that is so prevalent on Speak Up.

The slightly more serious tone and similarity of point of view of the authors may keep the big crowds away, though. It's Speak Up without the sense of humor, which is underlined by Design-Observer's gloomy design of white type on a black background. If only the authors of DesignObserver had combined their efforts with those of Speak Up, their respective strengths would have shown us the absolute best that graphic design has to offer, and the cross-pollination would have benefited everyone. Not to mention the fact that a single place to visit would greatly reduce the time spent on keeping up with all these different blogs.

I'M AWARE THAT MY ASSESSMENT of these blogs may be completely off the mark by the time this intro is published. The content and quality of blogs can change quickly, depending largely on who chooses to participate in the discussions. This points to one of the big differences between blogs and traditionally published magazines like *Emigre*. The essays we publish are usually the result of weeks or months of research and reflection. Blogs are like reality TV. They're fast paced and you get to find out exactly what's on people's minds right now, with all the pitfalls of a discussion forum without a moderator.

Yet, as I'm typing this, I wonder if design blogs like Speak Up and DesignObserver will make magazines such as *Emigre* obsolete, or at the very least replace our "Readers Respond" section. The open discussion format and instant feedback can be both entertaining and educational, presenting various points of view all at once, something traditional magazines can't offer.

Or will they simply implode? Most of these blogs are labors of love. They are free to join and virtually free of advertising. No revenue is generated. For a blog to remain successful, however, it must post new topics on a daily basis. These topics are usually presented in the form of short opinion pieces generated by a select number of authors. This takes effort and must weigh heavily against the regular jobs most authors have to make a living. It will be interesting to see how this will play out.

So far, however, these blogs have shown a lot of energy. Popular topics on Speak Up easily receive 20 to 30 posts within a few hours, with some topics running for days or weeks and generating over 200 postings.

ONE REASON A BLOG LIKE SPEAK UP attracts so many readers is that for the most part it's easy reading. It is no myth that many graphic designers have allergic reactions to design writing that is not immediately relevant to the practice of design or uses a form of writing they are unfamiliar with. This aversion is directed particularly at so-called "academic" writing, the kind that is usually created by design educators or scholars. Academic writing tends to be more difficult to read, as it tackles complex ideas, or looks at seemingly simple ideas and shows us that they're not. In terms of writing, it stands at the polar opposite of blog chatter.

It's difficult to determine which approach to writing about design is most effective or more important. It largely depends on what you are trying to accomplish. Design critic Rick Poynor, in a recent issue of *Print* magazine, looks at it this way: "...if design educators wish to bring about a more critically aware design profession, then it is up to them to talk to ordinary designers in a way designers can understand." Poynor is one of the most lucid writers around, and the clarity of his language rarely compromises the depth and scope with which he approaches his subject matter. His recently published book *No More Rules*, twice reviewed in this issue of *Emigre* (by Sam Potts and Lorraine Wild,), is the first book on postmodernism that I've read that does not require a post-graduate degree in literary theory and criticism to be fully understood.

Others, like David Cabianca (*see interview on page 63*) argue that we should be careful not to dumb-down our language in order to appease readers. Instead, we should challenge them. Cabianca, and Rob Giampietro in *Emigre* #64, both argue that, for design criticism to evolve, it must create its own language – a language not concerned with the lowest common denominator. This language, Cabianca says, "would borrow methods, theories, and concepts" used in "other disciplines, such as art theory, philosophy, comparative literature, American studies, and gender studies." This would require designers to familiarize themselves with these fields, and echoes Drenttel and Helfand's call for designers to expand their horizons.

My own vision of the perfect writer is of one who can write engagingly, has a distinct personal style, gives us new insights into our profession, and writes in a way that designers (and outsiders alike) can understand, yet challenges them intellectually. Of course such a writer can only exist if there is an appreciative audience and paying publications to support him/her.

It's unlikely this will ever happen. For design writing to thrive, we need to provide an environment in which writers can sharpen their skills on a full-time basis. For that to occur, we need to pay them a decent salary, and for that we need publications that can pay those salaries and disperse the writing. For that we need an appreciative audience, and for that we need good writers. It's a Catch 22.

I do, however, see a possibility for design blogs to help make the design profession more open to design writing and criticism. It's a medium made up primarily of text, which is a step in the right direction. And when those who discount the value of theory and criticism do so by writing down elaborate arguments against it, as is often the case on Speak Up, this tells me there's hope for design writing and theory.

Since a blog like Speak Up is open to everybody and has a growing audience, it provides a platform for aspiring writers to try out their ideas. Already, it has exposed a number of new voices of note; designers who obviously enjoy writing about design – who see it as a natural extension of their practice – and who can single-handedly raise the quality of the regular blog chatter. One of them, Sam Potts, a Speak Up author, makes his *Emigre* writing debut in this issue.

I just hope blogs won't go the way of digital music. People flock to stuff when it's free, and eventually expect everything to be free. And that's a deep hole to dig out of. *Emigre* had nearly 40,000 people requesting our magazine when subscriptions were free. When, in 2002, we went back to paid subscriptions, we barely hit the 2,000 mark. Changing our content to focus entirely on design writing didn't help circulation, either.

It would be a miracle, or the result of extreme dedication by certain individuals, if blogs such as Speak Up and DesignObserver could continue to exist free of charge and advertising. If they do, I hope that they'll keep pushing their writers to dig deeper and look at our profession from as many angles as possible. If we're lucky, they'll draw in some enthusiasts from outside the profession to broaden the discussion even further. But even if that doesn't work, with so much design chatter, at least for now, it feels a lot less lonely out here. RVDL

AN INTERVIEW
WITH ARMIN VIT.

———

DECEMBER 2003

Q | **Rudy VanderLans:** First I have to ask a somewhat silly question. Where did you learn to write so well? You were born in Mexico and went to school there. Grew up there, I presume. But your written English is impeccable.

A | **Armin Vit:** I've been in the U.S. for a little over four years and am just now starting to feel comfortable with my written English. My spoken English is quite good too, even though I have problems pronouncing words with *t*'s in the middle, like *button*, *tomato*, *little* and *Atlanta* — I usually have to look for replacement words. I took English courses on and off since I was eight years old, lots of grammar exercises. I just follow the rules I learned — don't ask me what the definition of a pronoun is, though. I now think in English instead of Spanish (as in making up grocery lists in my mind while showering).

Q | You and a few other Speak Up authors attended Portfolio Center. What is the single most important thing you learned there?

A | Actually, I did not attend Portfolio Center as a student, I was a teacher there for three quarters. I taught typeface design. My wife *did* attend their design program and is definitely the reason why we are having this conversation right now; otherwise I'd still be in Mexico. I "lived" the experience of being a student at Portfolio Center through her (late night trips to Home Depot included). The thing that most impressed me was the healthy competitiveness of the students, striving to learn about graphic design at all hours of the day. Hank Richardson's (dean of the school and head of the design program) energy and dedication is contagious. He never settles for anything, works twenty-four hours a day (almost literally), and expects the students to do the same. Most of them respond and it creates an environment full of creativity, responsibility, and, to my surprise, endless passion. As to the people who strut through Speak Up from Portfolio Center, I didn't know any of them personally at the time. Sam Potts was in my wife's class though, so I had some background information on him, and I knew he was a *design obsessionist* — a quality that can only be fostered by a place like Portfolio Center.

Q | What was the impetus for Speak Up? What ignited it? Were there other design blogs that you felt could be improved upon or that you were inspired by?

A | I so wish I already had a formulated answer for this, as it is the question I get asked most often. There are many factors that played a role in the impetus. First, and most objective, the original version of Speak Up was created during a cold Chicago winter, making it a labor that emerged from boredom and from me not willing to go outside and play in the snow. While the temperatures dropped, I started to develop a strong hatred towards "design portals" on the web, like K10K, Surfstation, and DiK (I'm over it now), and realized that there was no real website with useful links or information for graphic designers (not the eye-candy type). I think it was at that point I sort of had a "vision" of creating a collaborative website where *good* designers... I emphasize "good" because (a) the first people to whom I mentioned Speak Up were people like Bill Cahan, Sagmeister, Victore, and many more famous designers whose email addresses I was able to get a hold of, and (b) because I have always been a snob at heart. I got some nice words of encouragement but no participation, except from one friend, one stranger from Attik, my wife, and my wife's brother. Not the "boom" I had hoped for.

I let that version of Speak Up linger for a few months. Lingering turned into rotting and I was ready to sell my domain name on eBay. Then destiny breezed by and I ran into Typographica, a blog dedicated to all things relating to typography. Ironically, I got the link off K10K. Typographica was my first look at a blog of any kind. I then got invited as an author (thanks, Su) and quickly became addicted to the immediacy of the blog.

Typographica enjoyed a lot of success within the typographic community (regular contributors are Nick Shinn, Chester, Claudio Piccinini, and many more), and I figured that I could do the same within the graphic design community – which led to the current state of Speak Up.

On a more subjective level, the impetus rested more on the creation of a community for graphic designers where anyone could come in and feel inspired, challenged, motivated, or even depressed. I wanted to create a valuable tool, a reference and/or starting point for bigger things (ideas, thinking, what-have-you). I also felt a bit stuck myself. I was doing some interesting work from nine to five but after-hours I longed for more. I wasn't sure what it was then and I now know that Speak Up was just what I needed. Speak Up has challenged me intellectually, culturally, and socially. Hopefully it's doing the same for other people.

Q | How did you get the core group of Speak Up authors together? What are the criteria to become part of the core group? Will that list grow, or do you hope to keep it small?

A | When I launched the second version of Speak Up, I had no authors at all. It was just me. I put a call for authors on the front page. I had a small questionnaire for people to fill out online, and that way I was able to get a quick look at the background of those who were interested. I asked very basic questions: name, age, place of residence, occupation, kerning abilities, and, obviously, why they were interested in becoming authors. In the beginning I wasn't so finicky about the people I "hired" (I will use hire and fire for now, although I do not feel comfortable with those terms, but they help paint the picture). As I was looking to gather a list, I did tell a lot of people that our views differed, and many were offended. Of the first batch of authors I compiled, all, except Kiran Max Weber, are not part of Speak Up anymore. The majority just stopped contributing, others I fired.

Currently I am much, *much* more picky about whom I pick, and it is by invitation only, unless probed really hard by someone. I told you I was snobby at heart. The last five or six authors have come based on their participation on the site. Usually they are the ones making valuable contributions on a constant basis and are the ones bugging me (in the good meaning of the word) by email with ideas and suggestions for Speak Up. Some authors also come from controversy, just ask Debbie Millman. I sincerely believe that Speak Up would not be what it is if it weren't for most of the authors' participation, contributions, and continued belief in this venture. At this point I like the number of authors. I would like to keep it at this size with new authors replacing those whose involvement has dwindled a bit.

Q | Please explain the process by which you pick topics for Speak Up.

A | There are two major kinds of topics on Speak Up, under which fall all of the different categories. The first are those that represent the *now* of graphic design, like rebrandings of corporate identities, discussions on a certain lecture or conference, new line of computers by Apple — things that are happening at that exact moment and can be discussed, reviewed, critiqued, or laughed at with the immediacy that the web offers. The second kind of topics tends to be broader in scope and deeper, if you will, in meaning. Discussions ranging from spec work to portfolio do's and don'ts fall under this category. It is very important to me to keep the discussions related to graphic design. I have had many discussions with authors about bringing in other subjects like architecture or illustration. While these topics are interesting, and the way they are practiced relates to graphic design, I do not wish to be all things to all people. You want graphic design? You come to Speak Up. You want architecture? Start your own blog. As far as a process *per se*, there is none. If it's interesting, relevant, and can spark a good debate, it fits Speak Up. I do not review or edit (except for clarity or accuracy) any of the topics posted by authors. All of them have the autonomy to bring up any topic they feel like, even if sometimes I don't agree on the relevance.

Q | Speak Up is completely free of advertising. It's financed, supported, designed, and managed by you. It must take an enormous amount of your time. You also work at Norman Design. How are you able to juggle these two workloads?

A | The reason to keep Speak Up free of advertising was because banner ads (the excrement of the Internet) would completely ruin the design. Being self-sufficient makes the effort more valuable.

Q | What do you mean by that?

A | This is a personal trait. If my efforts come with no outside help (in this case, monetary help), I feel they have more merit because I did it all on my own. Sometimes when projects are harder to achieve, the results are more rewarding — at least for me. I don't like asking for help, even when I know I need it. But as we grow it is becoming apparent that some sort of funding might be necessary to make our projects a reality.

As far as workloads, it can sometimes become overbearing. I am *very* efficient though. Really. I don't waste my energies and am very organized. It comes from my dad. Just to give you a quick glance: I get to the office at eight in the morning, I do Speak Up (maintenance, start a topic, answer email, etc.) until nine, then I do some work until noon, half of my lunch hour goes to more Speak Up stuff and the other half for, well, lunch. After one in the afternoon, it's back to work until five (or after, depending on the workload and severity of deadlines), then I stay for another hour or more tending to Speak Up. I go home, and to my wife's dismay, I turn on the computer again to check that everything is OK. I like to take a break in the evenings, otherwise I will burn out quickly. The thing is, Speak Up has become a lifestyle for me (and my wife). I don't see it as something I *have* to do; I don't think of it as spending my *free time* on it. I spend that time petting the cats.

Q | Is Speak Up helping your design business in any way?
A | No, not really. Financially definitely not. It has certainly made us (specially me) more visible within the design community, but it's very unlikely it will get us any paying jobs.

Q | Because there's a core group of writers, Speak Up is often criticized for being cliquish. Do you have any concern that this may keep new people from joining the discussions?
A | Sometimes it does concern me. In the end, it is not necessarily my loss but that of those who choose not to jump in. Speak Up is completely open. There are no requirements in order to leave comments and take part in the discussion. There is obviously a stronger group of people within the site, even within the group of authors but, as this past year has proved, we are very open. I started this alone; everybody in the *clique* was at one point a newcomer.

Q | How have you kept Speak Up free of the kind of endless mudslinging and bickering that happens on some other blogs? Do you ever edit what comes in, or remove messages? Are you even able to edit? And at what point do you intervene, if at all?
A | Just to get the technical end clear: I am able to edit and remove comments. I can count the number of removed comments on only one hand. It usually is because of a personal, verbal attack on someone. I am not exactly sure what keeps the site free of the mudslinging you mention; the personable nature of the site makes it hard to be a complete ass. When it does happen, many of the regular contributors publicly make a point of it being a waste of time. It's an unacknowledged, unspoken pact we have developed. You also see real names as opposed to the usual, rather immature

and stupid, nicknames. The level of the overall language also sets the tone for the site and this, again, is because of all the participants. To be honest, I am as surprised as you are that there isn't as much "web immaturity" as expected.

Q | Do you have any idea of how many people currently visit Speak Up on a daily basis?

A | As opposed to other design-related web administrators, I won't lie about my stats. I receive between 275 to 300 unique visitors a day. I have had as many as 500 in a day. Overall hits is a different issue; these can range anywhere between 5,000 and 10,000 a day. I like that it's a small audience. I like to think of Speak Up as one of the best kept secrets on the web for graphic designers.

Q | What would you like to tell designers who may be sitting behind their Macs ready to post a message on Speak Up, but are perhaps a bit self-conscious or simply nervous posting their thoughts on such a public forum?

A | Honestly? Just fucking do it. There is no reason strong enough not to post. I won't lie either, we *will* bite. But their (your) opinion is as important as anyone else's. We want to hear it, discuss it, agree and disagree with it, have some fun with it, and hopefully learn something from it. We are all putting ourselves in the exact same position. We are all vulnerable and empowered at the same time.

Q | Lorraine Wild recently called Speak Up a "significant platform" for design but as a design historian, she is sad that it exists in a medium that is impermanent. I guess she is concerned about all that material disappearing over time. What are your plans, if any, to catalog and preserve all this dialog?

A | The first eight months of Speak Up have been properly catalogued. Every post, or entry, has been formatted in Microsoft Word, and all of them have been labeled with a code relating to an entry number, author, category, and title. I have four binders so far with all the printed material, along with one CD with files. I have to do it more regularly, though. Also, the back-end system can export *all* of it in one single file; I do that every month.

Q | A few weeks back you posted a lengthy critique where you wrote that "Speak Up is not just mine anymore." It sounded like you were overwhelmed, and that Speak Up had taken on a life of its own. Is it difficult to steer Speak Up?

A | Actually, the context in which I wrote it was to point out that any critiques of Speak Up are now directed at all the people who participate in it, not only me. But your question is very much on target; there are many times when I feel overwhelmed by the twists Speak Up takes on its own. More specifically, the quote you just mentioned came after a very thorough critique of what the site has become (in tone, focus, and its "agenda"), which was started by one of our authors and it opened some gates I would have rather stayed shut. I couldn't control it for a few days. I actually didn't even comment on the discussion; people had things they wanted to say and nothing I could have said or done would have stopped them. Speak Up does have a life of its own, but I like to believe that I am still in control — after all, I am the only one who can shut it off at any given time.

Q | Your recent promotional booklet for Speak Up, the one you passed out at the AIGA conference in Vancouver, is titled *Stop Being Sheep*. Can you explain what you mean by that title, and how it relates to Speak Up?

A | We did not start out with that title and we owe Kenneth FitzGerald for inspiring it. As we perused all the comments, we ran across one from Kenneth where he finished with that sentence. We loved it and felt it was appropriate to represent Speak Up's first year. Speak Up encourages each person to express their opinions, share their experiences, and basically say whatever they want to whomever they want. Challenging the (excuse me for this but I have to say *"status quo"* at some point in my career) *status quo* is not something that's going to happen by being a follower; change will not happen without individualism. The profession needs more unique, strong voices. I believe Speak Up can foster them.

Q | In *Stop Being Sheep*, you wrote "Speak Up stresses and questions the importance of the profession in our culture. It challenges those who practice inside the field, in hope of more accountability for their actions and in light of the responsibility we all have as communicators." In Speak Up threads, this accountability and responsibility seems to relate mostly to the client's bottom line. In other words, if, let's say, a branding campaign increased the client's profits, the design is considered successful. Do you think that a client's profits is the best way to measure how successful we are as communicators and the effect we have on our culture?

A | I wouldn't say it is the best or only way. It is indeed the most tangible and measurable. Is it the best way to measure the efforts of our profession? Definitely not, but it should not be completely disregarded, either. As a graphic designer, I first feel responsible for my client and making sure that what I propose affects their business in a positive way — financially as well as culturally.

Q | Tell me if I'm wrong, but the general theme of Speak Up and the belief of its most vocal authors is that whatever the marketplace dictates, goes. In other words, graphic design is primarily a service profession, entirely beholden to business and commerce. The sense I get from this is that design only has relevance, or becomes more relevant, when applied to serious for-profit businesses. Do you agree with that?

A | I agree with graphic design being a service profession. I don't agree with the marketplace dictating how graphic design evolves, but it would be unrealistic to think it doesn't. I also disagree with design being beholden to business or commerce. Graphic design is a response, as well as a reflection, of culture, politics, and art. The fact that we get paid (handsomely in some cases) for our service makes design easy to dismiss as nothing but decoration for business and commerce. I may be the wrong person (as I have done very little of it) to preach about the importance of doing work for non-profit organizations, but I think it is important and every designer should try it at least once in their careers. However, I don't think it's more or less relevant — or *better* or *worse* for that matter — than doing work for for-profit businesses.

Q | The word "relevance" comes up often in regard to certain design-
ers. You have mentioned that you admire designers such as
Ed Fella or Elliott Earls, but that you don't see the "relevance"
of their work. What exactly do you mean by that? What is it that
their work should be relevant to?

A | I knew I was digging myself a hole with those statements. I admire
both of these designers' work immensely. Both have influenced
my way of thinking about design further than stylistic treatments.
I think their relevance doesn't stretch as far as I would hope.
I wish it did. Shit, I wish I could stretch it myself and somehow
work it into my commerce-beholden work. Maybe it's just me and
my inability to channel their vision into mainstream, but I don't
think it will succeed. Their work is relevant for me, for many
designers, and for design history. There is no denying that. Yet
that's where their relevance ends: in a closely knit circle of
professionals.

Q | Some of the lengthiest and feistiest discussions on Speak Up seem
to center on logos. The logos of UPS, Burger King, VH1, Lee Jeans,
etc., sparked endless debates. If someone from outside our
profession accidentally stumbled across Speak Up, they might

think that the most important thing in graphic design is logo design. Why do designers put such importance on logos?

A | I'll start by stating that I, personally, think a logo is the most important thing in graphic design. It is the epitome of what a graphic designer can do, which is distilling the most complex and varied information into a single communication element. One reason I think a lot of people have gotten so upset about the rebranding efforts you mentioned is because they are disregarding (they might call it "challenging") most of the notions of what a logo is. It is true that a company's logo nowadays is only a small part of the overall branding effort, yet I think designers are using it as a very easy excuse to create poorly executed logos. Maybe ten, twenty years from now we will no longer put such high expectations on a logo (since that is what most designers have been taught all their lives), because we will all expect the rest of the branding efforts to make up for a lazy designer's indifference to the importance of a logo. Isn't it interesting, though, that logo discussions get so heated? I never saw it coming either, yet it does clearly reflect the significance that logos have for designers. More than we all thought.

Q | A few months back you were very explicit about not giving a hoot about specifying recycled paper, using soy-based ink, or making economic use of paper. You said, "Why should I make a big effort for the environment when 95% of America is wasting so much fucking stuff?" And in a recent thread you were very cynical about the AIGA's National Conference themes, some of which focused on sustainability, recycling, etc. You said: "If they start preaching about hugging trees I will be very disappointed. I can join Green Peace for that and in return get a cool green jacket." Don't you think that the responsibility and accountability that we have as designers, as you bring up in *Stop Being Sheep*, extends to how we use resources?

A | It does. Definitely. It may very well be the single most important issue that I don't espouse as much as I should. I'm going to sound like a horrible person, but this issue is something I'm not that concerned about. Don't get me wrong, I don't go out on the street throwing garbage and spraying my hair to make the ozone hole bigger. I just channel my energies in different ways. Perhaps I need to change. Nobody has to convince me. I know that I could make a difference (albeit very small). I just need to convince myself.

Q | You greatly admire a designer such as Stefan Sagmeister for his guts and often shocking design. Yet at the same time you have said that "Right now is not a good time to experiment. At least not with a client's projects. There is too much fragility involved to be messing with somebody else's business to satisfy the design critics who want to crack open the next big thing." When a designer aspires to do something challenging, something unique, something that will turn heads and truly differentiate a client, like Sagmeister often does, isn't that what design is supposed to do? Isn't that the best way to serve a client and our culture?

A | Yes, that's what we all aspire to in the end. Within the turning-heads-to-truly-differentiate-a-client approach to design there can be many variations. Sagmeister's shock technique could be labeled as experimental for the sake of this question. His commercial work takes many risks that I would never take with a client. Maybe it's my insecurity, maybe it's my understanding of my clients' needs. Whatever the reason is, I do not feel comfortable (right now) to take such risks. Another variation of the turning-head approach is work by — brace yourself, I'm going to the complete opposite — Landor. Their work can have a similar effect (BP's and FedEx's logos do it for me) abiding by more *conventional* ways.

Q | Rick Poynor in *Eye* has mentioned that "something new may be emerging" with Speak Up. If that is so, do you think Speak Up represents any kind of new *zeitgeist* within graphic design? If yes, what would that *zeitgeist* be?

A | I tend to be on the humble side usually, yet I will have to unabashedly and proudly admit that, yes, Speak Up does represent a kind of *zeitgeist*, even if I would never call it that myself. There has never been a forum with the immediacy and response of Speak Up. Part of that success is the instantaneous nature of the web, but I would not attribute it only to that. The discussions and issues on Speak Up literally reflect the spirit of our time and our profession. We could easily rest on that quality alone but we do go further — questioning, critiquing, attacking, defending, giving these issues importance and relevance. Today, tomorrow, every single day.

Q | While we were working on this interview, a new design blog was started called DesignObserver, run by Bill Drenttel, Jessica Helfand, Rick Poynor, and Michael Bierut. Those are some big name, heavyweight design writers. Do you see this as a competing blog, or do you see this as an opportunity to further distinguish the goal of Speak Up?

A | There are too many similarities to not consider it competition. We are both vying for (graphic design) readers' attention on the Internet, I guess, and looking to further the discourse in our profession. We are each doing it our own different way, much like Charles Barkley and Larry Bird played the same sport with very different approaches and personalities — in this analogy Speak Up is Charles Barkley, of course. But in the end I am not sure what ultimate prize (fame, fortune?) we would be competing for, so I don't think I see them as competition, exactly. Life is more fun when you have somebody else to measure up (or down) against. It keeps you on your toes, striving for more, and, like you said, it is an opportunity to distinguish Speak Up as a consistent offering of fresh, unbiased, challenging dialogue.

Q | Has Speak Up changed your own ideas about graphic design in any
way? If yes, what has been the most significant change?

A | Definitely. There are a lot of preconceptions I had on various topics
that have been changed, mostly because I had never had such
open discussions with so many points of view with so many
people. It is hard to pinpoint exact instances, but for example,
I used to be more preoccupied with winning awards than I am
now. I think the biggest change has come in the form of what
graphic design in general means to me; three years ago I was only
concerned with finding the right typeface to go with a logo and
creating good-looking stuff; now I think about graphic design
in a bigger way. Why are we doing what we are doing? How are we
furthering culture? How can we become better? And I know the
answer is not tucked away in a font menu.

Q | How does it feel to become the center of attention and have every-
thing you say get thrown back at you?

A | I won't lie: I love it. I don't do any of this for the attention (I would
miss it if it went away, though). It has been a nice side-effect of
this whole ordeal. It has given me opportunities that wouldn't
happen otherwise. To start with, I would not be writing this right
now. I have been able to have conversations with many of the
people I admire – an opportunity I wouldn't have without this
attention. It's overwhelming at times; the question of *why me?*
is always in the back of my mind. Weirdest thing is that I'm one
of the shyest and quietest people you will ever meet but, like
I have said before, I'm feisty behind the keyboard.

Having everything I say thrown back in my face is threatening
as well as encouraging. It makes me think harder about what I
want to say and how to say it. I tend to contradict myself sometimes, but I don't see that as a problem (I think Paul Rand was
a great contradictor himself). I look forward to the challenges that
this brings. I aspire to people calling me on my shit; otherwise it
would be too boring.

I COME TO BURY GRAPHIC DESIGN, NOT TO PRAISE IT.

KENNETH FITZGERALD

TO CONSIDER HOW TO TEACH or theorize about graphic design, a basic question must be answered: what is its ultimate goal? Ideally, that answer will be less abstract than the platitude, "to make the world a better place." However, for the purpose of this discussion, I'll agree that improving life is one of design's ambitions. It's just not design's primary objective. An impulse precedes it that is truly primal.

Already I, like many other commentators, have described design as having intent, as a species might. If design behaves with such self-awareness, its essential impulse is to perpetuate itself. In other words, with apologies for the pun, its first concern is reproduction. This motivation is often to the exclusion of better-place-making the world. Most theory – whether it is "academic" or "practical" – also comes down to procreation: assuring the creation of more professional design.

To assure its existence, design strives to create a class of expert professional practitioners with high social standing. The archetype that designers emulate is the architect. Unfortunately, there hasn't yet been an Ayn Rand with a 1,000-page novel about a heroic information architect who plays by their own rules.

While ostensibly desiring awareness of and recognition for its activity, design deliberately makes little real substantive effort to reach out to non-designers to explain what it's doing and why. Instead, it incessantly argues that design professionals should be given more work. And the arguments are aimed inward. For instance, there's the AIGA's recent 12-step booklet with the poignant question "Why?" on its cover. It's another demonstration of simultaneous affirmation ("we're influential!") and denial (preaching to the converted).

While an elevated status would benefit practitioners, a cadre of design specialists may not be the best condition. Do we desire a society permanently estranged from its visual expression? Is mediation perfection? Do we seek to extinguish the vernacular?

We should be resigned to never achieving full regard for expert design production. The reason is that as the non-designer public become converts to design's message, the conversion is total. The design connoisseur will become a designer – and by all measures, a good one, too. The situation is analogous to why it's impossible to surpass the speed of light. The additional energy that is input to increase acceleration is progressively converted to mass. The faster you go, the closer you get and the more weighed down you become. Likewise, a broader and deeper appreciation of design can – and should – only lead to its demise as a specialist profession.

A thorough appreciation of design should elicit the desire to do it yourself. Isn't this where little designers come from? It's also the ultimate purpose of all the arts. We seek a society where everyone is making art, being creative. Increasing access to the means of

PRODUCTION + DESIRE = AN EXPLOSIVE MIX.

But if everyone's an artist, then no one is. So, too, would designers be everywhere and nowhere.

A high profile example of conversion is Rem Koolhaas. The controversial architect was evidently so taken by Bruce Mau's productions that he got into the game and formed his own design studio. Koolhaas now self-directs slabs of cool architectural theory like *The Harvard Guide to Shopping*. He also devised a Hue-PC flag for the European Union, which deliberately refers in form to bar codes. Of course, trained graphic designers are doing the heavy lifting, with Koolhaus as art director. The works are contemporary, capable, and forgettable. Koolhaus's engagement in design might be considered another triumph for the field. It is, in fact, a sign of the coming apocalypse.

Another recent non-designer celebrity is former Mac temp Dave Eggars. Though he only designs for his limited edition *McSweeney's* literary journal and associated products (such as David Byrne's pseudo-Bible *The New Sins*), Eggars was selected for the second National Design Museum Triennial. Apart from attempting to siphon off some of his media velocity, the choice is puzzling.

Eggars's approach is an anti-design style, flouting professional treatment. Issues of *McSweeney's* are dense with classically readable text, set solely in Garamond. Monotony is relieved by goofing about with cover typography and altering the issues' forms. Never has a strategy so outwardly minimal been so showy and indulgent. The design is clever but no more so than numerous 'zines — except for the producer's notoriety. Honoring Eggars seems less a pronunciation of design's significance than an expression of self-loathing.

Interest in "undesigned" design has also increased recently. This approach isn't anti-design, as it doesn't mock the field's concerns. It is puritan, invoking what is thought of as an essential form purged of visual rhetoric and subjectivity. Rob Giampietro recently critiqued the prevalent undesigned design, "default systems design," in *Emigre* 65. Here, an automatized design format has been widely adopted as a standard. Determined more by production software than intention, it establishes a vernacular by Adobe or Quark fiat. Giampietro rightly points out that investigating the origin and meaning of these systems is a vital concern for design.

A surprising instance of attention to the undesigned is in the second edition of *Graphic Design: A Concise History*. Richard Hollis concludes his book by highlighting a design without designers. It isn't a forum where you'd expect the unprofessional to be championed. And it's not. Hollis cites examples of information design: "Paradoxically, the 1999 book *Open Here: The Art of Instructional Design*...drew attention to diagrams and instructions prepared without the intervention of 'designers'."

Hollis then muses acidly on designerlessness: "The world may yet dispense with the profession while designers are arguing about whether they are artists or not." His interest in undesigner activity is confined to its effect on work he loathes. Perhaps he dares to hope that modernist design principles have been fully assimilated into culture. However, the risk encompasses even design Hollis endorses.

Though from a different perspective, I agree that untrained design can make inroads into information design. This might be considered the branch of design impervious to unprofessional interloping. But we should consider the example of Edward Tufte, as practitioner and in practice. His route into design shows design training isn't necessary for someone to be considered a genius of information design. But in practice, his methods show flaws, as in the discussion of the Challenger shuttle disaster in *Visual Explanations*. Tufte shows the poor diagramming of O-Ring temperature performance data and suggests professional design might have averted the tragedy.

However, Tufte fails to account for the subjective realities of culture – culture as broad social forces and as smaller group dynamics. Recently, for instance, it was shown how the culture within NASA – which would seem a wholly objective, rational institution – made the efficacy of diagrams irrelevant. As the Columbia accident investigation once again demonstrated, the relations within NASA made for curious and fatal reinterpretations of data. Managers could interpret a professionally perfect diagram of excessive risk as normative – just as they redefined the ongoing threat of falling ice as a benign nuisance.

Design culture is similarly blind to its motivations. If we imagine graphic design as an individual, we must explain why it doesn't affirm its desired identity, then breed wildly. My explanation is Freudian: design has a death wish. It constantly seeks to eradicate itself.

Designers will instinctively reject this notion. We're fighting for our lives! Indulgent clients are at a premium. Remedies are hard sought, sometimes extreme. In a 1995 column for *I.D.* magazine, "In Search of the Perfect Client," Michael Bierut suggested we might have to psychologically condition future employers from childhood. "Why not," he asked, "find an artistically-inclined 10-year-old who might otherwise choose a design career...establish them on the corporate fast track, and wait for this 'mole' to become CEO of a major corporation?" Elsewhere, Bierut seems to insinuate that genetic engineering is the answer.

Bierut's proposal is facetious but the situation is serious. Decades of famous graphic designers have practiced, ones esteemed for their skills in communication and persuasion, yet still designers bemoan their impotence. I offer this without sarcasm. Design continues to contain prodigious talents and intellects. What's wrong with this picture? The answer's not in *I.D.*, it's the id.

The foremost sign of design's Thanatos compulsion is its bipolar relationship with the vernacular. Here is design's ultimate poison pill. It's popped regularly – but in prophylactic sub-critical doses. For some designers, it's an elixir, to vitalize. For others, it's an inoculation, providing immunity.

Self-identified modernists and fellow travelers habitually scorn the vernacular and any designer having truck with it. In a 2002 letter to *Eye*, "Anglosaxonic" designer Robin Fior wrote: "A keen vernacular relativist like Mr. FitzGerald could surely paste the 'just visiting jail' icon from the Monopoly board alongside the bars, and Bob's your uncle." While the meaning of the statement continues to elude me, I'm 100% certain it has a mueca of distaste for all-inclusive.

To detractors, vernacular design is crude, subjective, and...well, often I'm not quite sure why. It's puzzling how individuals proclaiming devotion to the dissemination of texts could so loathe its spontaneous expressions. Or find value in them. The inevitable result of their disdain is public suspicion of design. Designers are widely seen as possessing an elitist aesthetic agenda insensitive to people's needs. (To be fair, anti-modernists, while not present at the creation, haven't substantially countered the perception.)

Isn't there a disconnect between advocating the free flow of information but allowing only a clique of specialists to direct it? The modernist rejection of the vernacular may come from recognizing the true risk to designers. It's not that commerce – the public exchange of ideas, goods, and services – will be stultified without professional design, but that it will go on quite well, thank you. And that very little of the design everyday people respond to looks like work they champion.

Meanwhile, design also has a fascination with and frequently embraces the vernacular. It's a bracing reality check for over-theorized design. Someone needs to make a sign and they just make it. Appreciating vernacular speech is an inspirational experience of humility.

However, in its passion, design stalks contemporary art and "outsider art." We have no verdict if these romances represent appreciation or abuse. The uncritical use of vernacular sources has received extensive critique. Cultural exploitation and aesthetic sloth are regular appraisals.

In his 1994 pamphlet *Fellow Readers*, Robin Kinross rightly discerns another motive: "...in another move...against the threat of redundancy, the fad for vernacular bad taste may be an attempt by designers to survive by blending into the landscape, chameleon-like." Here are designers abandoning their identity, acting on the death wish. Yet after delivering this insight, Kinross immediately follows with a questionable conclusion: "These strategies must be doomed by their own bad faith, if not by public indifference to them." The public popularity of work like Charles Anderson's contests the latter part of the statement (unless we dismiss him as "primarily a North American phenomenon"). And to the former, it's an unfortunate cynicism that decries when it must descry.

Of course, the boundaries of what constitutes "colloquial speech" are variable. As in the work of Charles Anderson, it can be an anachronistic commercial art that meets all the tests of professional product. The distinctions are irrelevant. What is significant is that designers look outside their professional standard to a source considered pure and immediate. And, often — from hand-drawn and painted signage to 'zines to desktop horrors no designer would uphold — distressingly effective.

DESIGN EDUCATION IS WHERE "little designers" come from. Yet despite its total allegiance to the profession – even in the renowned/ reviled "progressive" and "experimental" programs – the importance of education is still given only lip service in the field. The notion that design is an on-the-job learning experience continues to dominate. Students enter with a vague interest in text and image – often, not even that – and are channeled wholesale into professional design making. A successful design program is defined as one that (re)produces more professional design and designers. What other measure is there?

There is the accumulation of knowledge for its own sake: the goal of the liberal arts. Gordon Salchow wrote "Graphic Design is not a Profession" ten years ago for the *AIGA Journal*. He pointed out design's resemblance to literature and music, calling design a "...fundamental humanist communications discipline...its peers are the Liberal Arts."

Gunnar Swanson's furthered it in his 1994 *Design Issues* essay "Graphic Design Education as a Liberal Art: Design and Knowledge in the University and the 'Real World'." He speculated about studying graphic design without the intention of actually practicing it. "Can studying design be of general, not just professional, interest?" Swanson asked, "Do we really have anything to offer outside of the sometimes questionable promise of a job?"

Andrew Blauvelt critiqued this proposition in notes to Will Novosedlik's 1996 *Eye* article, "Dumb." "Design as a field of study without practical application is unlikely and undesirable...it is the practice of graphic design that provides the basis of a theory of graphic design." Swanson's idea was to him merely a "quest for academic legitimacy." He promotes a "'critical making,' teaching when, how and why to question things."

Blauvelt's counterpoint is so terse (likely from space considerations) that it's difficult to speculate overmuch on it. However, it is completely in line with the prevalent professional viewpoint.

It's also surprisingly self-deprecating when comparing design to "true" liberal arts. Blauvelt's move from academia to making is notable in this regard.

He's right that design educators are on a quest for legitimacy, though not in the surreptitious sense he means. Design education should strive for the idealism of education. Actually, matters are much better than I am presenting them. Every time I encounter a designer complaining of the "theoretical" and "impractical" projects they were assigned in college, I know they likely studied under a teacher who recognizes an educator's responsibility.

Blauvelt is also correct that, at present, design study without application is unlikely. Academia promotes design education the way the field likes it — as practical. The attitude isn't part of some conspiracy, just a mirroring of societal attitudes. But Swanson's article makes no suggestion to dissociate from practice. Just that some students might find design study of interest while not intending to go on to a career of professional making. In the article, Swanson readily acknowledges problems with his proffer: "Currently, there is no clear role for design scholarship." Subsequently, he has identified the most profound flaw: who will teach the design side of this curriculum? How many design-savvy educators are open to this approach — and have the breadth and depth of knowledge to succeed at it?

There is an oversight in Blauvelt's critique that is reflexive for designers. For them, design education is entirely about producing designers. It's vocational training. There's nothing wrong with that — unless you're claiming to be engaged in something else. Swanson, however, is discussing education, in a design context.

Here is a real world certainty every design educator must confront: the majority of design students will not go into professional practice. What is our responsibility to them? Does design care about anything other than producing more design(ers)?

An education *through* design rather than *in* design should be our goal. If that's not possible, what does it say for all the claims of design's significance to and in the world? Is design just for designers? A shift in education away from a professional emphasis may also benefit students dedicated to a career of making. Designers claim their activity is all about ideas — not software, not formal facility. Educators are called upon to foster a critical sensibility: a questioning mind capable of intellectual discipline. Design's vital aspect of craft is a product of a cognitive awareness. The hand does not move of its own accord, either to move a mouse or pull a trigger.

A liberal arts model isn't a magical solution. There are numerous practical hazards in academia. How it puts that idealistic pursuit into practice — education as menu of courses — is a major concern. Well-funded design programs being hijacked or infiltrated by sinecure seekers is another. And what do we do for research institutions and art schools? A liberal arts model may also exacerbate the anti-intellectualism rampant in the field. To be at all cerebral as a designer automatically brings the designation of being a "pseudo-intellectual." Just as any design critique that's not a case study is "theoretical"; i.e., irrelevant.

We might smile at Michael Bierut's proposal, but where are those future patrons going to come from? Designers occasionally talk about "educating the client." But if designers are so dismissive of their education — by designers — what makes them think clients will take lessons? Here's a cliché: the future of design's too important to leave to the designers. Just as the profession can't form a critical writing, it's unable to best represent its own interests.

We're arguably at a saturation point, even with an improved economy. (Never mind the influx of new designers.) Designers need to convert the mass of people who have the economic means to hire designers but don't believe there's an advantage in doing so. The main strategy so far hasn't been to craft an argument, but an imitation.

Design constructed itself as professional service — formal speech

— to commune with industry. Business styles itself as rational, tangible, and methodical. But a glance at any day's business news shows that those are affectations. Enron is the rule, not the exception. Mismanagement, indecision, and fantasy are the prevalent attributes. Corporate America is as much an ego-fueled crapshoot as design is. The relationship between business and design is prickly because of the similitude.

Still, design strives to be taken seriously on the business playing field. The desultory drive for certification in the 1990s was part of this drive. Its ebbing is another hesitation mark on design's wrist. The effort failed less from active resistance than indifference. The claimed benefits were never substantiated and everyone was too busy trying to make a living to work it out. Certification addresses a professional existence — design as vocation. Design is just a job to most of its practitioners. The majority of studios and corporate art departments are factories. How would certification rectify this?

I've previously suggested that the AIGA should reconstitute itself as a union. The circumstances of a design job — from employment security to conceptual self-determination — won't improve without organized action. If designers believe they are vital, how about organizing a strike to demonstrate it?

Professionalizing design is a mechanism to cover the bizarre nature of the activity. Design is a dislocated art form born out of industrialization. The idea of professional artists is fairly implausible, certainly as a way to consistently generate fresh insight. The activity inevitably becomes routinized and formulaic when required to be on demand. The product turns distant, abstract, and impersonal. Yes, there are exceptions, but they're rare. Instead, we get a lot of admirable, formally accomplished work. To paraphrase Oscar Wilde, they are works of talent, not genius.

The simple truth is that professional design will almost always fall short of touching hearts because it's second-hand love. Designers love doing design, the client is just a vehicle. (This is why the slur that designers are prostitutes is flat wrong. But is it better to be a sex addict?) Design is like a Cyrano de Bergerac who speaks irresistible words of love because of a passion for language. Roxane he can take or leave. If design loves anyone, it's Baron Christian.

It's no mystery that the most celebrated, expressive, and inspiring design is either self-motivated or when the designer is truly empowered and entrusted. You must have a personal stake. This is the norm. It's the itinerant artist model that's an aberration. Why else do designers have creative side projects to, as they describe it, gratify their creative urges? Shouldn't this tell them that they're in the wrong business? Or that design shouldn't be a business? (This does not mean, however, that designers must only do design.) Maybe design should be left to people inspired by the nutrition labels on food packages.

"Blending into the landscape" is the only responsible action for design. Design must join the culture and abandon attempts to seduce, party with, or ride herd on it. Those projects are doomed to failure, as they should be. The results of the modernist program – decay into formal gestures, creation of "merely a designer-culture" – are a proof. (There is no postmodern program.)

These are not theoretical wanderings. They arise from reading designers' relentless laments about the unappreciated, unrewarding aspects of their pursuit. If it's to be more than unfocused bitching, some fundamental assumptions must be challenged. A truth to be faced is that the only problem professional design solves with any demonstrable success is a designer's urgency to get a professional design job.

Professionalism has reigned supreme throughout design's existence – there's nothing else to blame. To have change, design must change. This is a tall order – to go out on an edge, peering into the unknown. Whether we continue the course of professional determination or alternative conceptions of design, in the words of David Lee Roth, you might as well jump.

Jump!

Kenneth FitzGerald is an Assistant Professor of Art at Old Dominion University in Norfolk, Virginia. This is a revised version of a paper presented at *Design: Refining Our Knowledge*, an international graphic design education conference, held at the University of Minnesota in October 2003.

MUTE

BEN HAGON

There are no voices, only producers.

————

Critical design writing circa 2003 is in crisis. "Visual Communications Specialists" continue to reproduce faster than horny rats, yet new voices and new ideas, are scarce. As a result, our days are as dull as the work we produce, and our relevance, both cultural and commercial, dies.

The old guard of design writing – Rick Poynor, Steven Heller, Jessica Helfand, and Ellen Lupton – continue to stimulate the brain, yet rarely do we see new names printed on the pages of our favorite rags. My fear is that as the Poynors retire, so will critical thought. Are young bucks happy to accept the general level of bullshit that a professional has to tolerate on a daily basis from clients, co-workers, and bosses? "Enlarge the logo, change Pantone 811 to our blue, and put it all in Times New Roman – that's what we've always done."

Sure we are here for our clients, and we understand that they know their audience: they are the boss. But does this mean that, as designers, we must do as we are told? Clients should be coming to us for our technical skills and our knowledge, but if we don't question or think – only produce – what knowledge can we claim to offer?

I'll go as far as to say that designers are actively discouraged from thinking. Instead we are taught to be "creative." "Here's the brief, here are the requirements and limitations, whip me up something clever and beautiful!" This dumbly linear approach to a supposedly progressive profession is not only boring, it's harmful to our future. If we don't look deeper into the process of what we produce, the end result will never be innovative or even interesting. What we produce will merely be well-executed versions of what has been done before.

Yes, there are dissenting voices here and there. They're ignored. Instead of living and changing with the questions and tensions created by *Adbusters* and First Things First 2000, designers are content to dismiss them as idealistic, unrealistic, Commie bullshit. We are more apt to cuddle up to old faithful Pentagram, and spit-polish our Yellow Pencils.

Admittedly, when one's whole system is being called into question it is intimidating. But we must rise to the challenge instead of sinking further into the stinky morass of self-celebration that began with the "superstar" designer culture in the late-1980s.

Denise Gonzales Crisp describes the trend of "Big D-design" in "Visitations": "The only goal is to create appropriate solutions to any so-called problem created by a client...This kind of work must always look like design, rather than by contrast, looking like, well, something informed by other things than graphic design!" [1] If we designers did what we learned at school — to look for inspiration in people, arts, architecture, technology, dialogue, philosophy, the world at large, as opposed to reverting to design magazines and hard-covered, case-bound testimonials — we would become original once again. Our design would stop being Design (neo-modernism) and begin to represent and interact with the world around us. Which would make us more relevant to the socio-cultural make-up of our communities, as opposed to only being quantitatively valuable to our potential clients. By using outside sources to influence our work — Macmonkeys, get away from your desk — our field may have some effect besides selling chocolate bars, lawyers, and easy chairs.

Appropriation syndrome.

———

"Style vs. content" is irrelevant. It is obvious to designers that today's work needs both an idea — or that most grossly of overused terms, a concept — and a style to garner any real success. Whether the work favors style or content is not the issue. The issues are: Which clients do we work with? Which ones do we refuse to work with? By what method do we reach our end product? How do we produce new, relevant work? Without asking these questions, design will not evolve. Our obsession with the style/surface/results of our work and an ever-present quest for fame (dressed up as recognition) is stunting progress.

So we keep solving our client's so-called problems in the same way designers have been doing for over 50 years. Modernism's fundamental design idiom – "content" displayed "clearly" with little interference from "style" – remains today's major design method.

But this type of design is not a philosophy, it's a mere formula. Steven Heller, in his book *Less is More*, predicted in 1999 that "Simplicity means a return to basics but not at the expense of excitement."[2] Not true; what we now see are acres of white space, finely chosen photography/illustration and plenty of "well-set" type (often gray, in 7 pt.).

Herein lies the major problem. Since this formula has existed for over half a century, most clients will be at the very least somewhat versed in the vernacular. And so clients believe they know design, and the formula for successful design, which therefore leads to the crisis we now face: "Can you make that bigger and bleed this bit?"

When clients declare that they want their piece to look cool/elegant/edgy, the designer's red flag should be immediately raised. With this statement, the client is indicating that they already know what they want; they just can't execute it. We are demoted from creatives to production-line labor. Or worse, clients think they know what will work (for them), but can't express it, which in turn sets the chosen designer up for complete failure.

The continued practice of appropriating what has gone before – plus our lack of meaningful thought and discussion – will make us, as creatives, redundant. If all we do is reproduce styles from the past (while integrating our clever "concepts"), designers will become little more than Mac operators. The client will give the order: "Our company is built upon strong values, please make our brochure look like a piece of Rodchenko's work. Here's the text, have it done by Thursday at four." If we do not begin to work in a way that continues design's evolution instead of the postmodern, appropriation rut we find ourselves in, design, like all non-evolving entities, will die.

It's our own fault.

There is safety in what has gone before: if a design method worked for the X account then it will for the Z account. Blame does not rest with the client; they're just doing their job. The responsibility is the designers' and creative directors'. If we let repetitive, generic solutions be reproduced while the checks roll in, then we are squarely to blame.

If you do it my way, it is possible you may enjoy a smidgen of the success I enjoy.

The design era of 1996 to today could be called the monograph years. These egoists' crutches are stunting the growth of design. A culture of hero worship prevents young designers from approaching design differently. If all a new designer has as inspiration is somebody else's work or approach to work, he or she cannot be expected to think originally. When the industry finally focuses on critical thinking over idolatry, more original approaches – and better designers – will surface.

Monographs are even more disturbing when dressed up as socially aware, as in Bruce Mau's *Life Style*. Robert Fulford, in his essay "All Hail Mau the Magnificent," puts it into perspective: "Whatever Mau's message it's overwhelmed by his medium...Those who make the effort to read it will discover they are spending all this time on an elaborate exercise in self-congratulation, a designer's promotional piece."[3] Other monographs, such as Scher's *Make it Bigger* and Kalman's *Perverse Optimist*, are equally disgusting. Pity should be assigned to newcomers in this climate. It is almost impossible to uncover truly fresh, original work.

Not tomorrow.

———

The time for revolution is now. The appropriation years are fast approaching their tenth year anniversary. Ten years is often the duration of a cultural habit — see punk, hippy, cubism, 80s new wave, etc. If we push through modernism's outdated rules and formulas and run with something functional, something with legs, then design will evolve once again.

Design could live up to its threat of being a vehicle for cultural expression. Much like literature or cinema has been in the past, design could represent culture at a ground level. Whereas cinema and literature have an exaggerated way of revealing what is happening around us, design could be a true representation of our times. Without the aid of flattering lighting or make-up artists, our messages could help frame the world we live in, instead of merely perpetuating the airbrushed, bleached teeth, Martha Stewart Inc. myth.

Change or die.

———

Choose men and women of all colors, shapes, and sizes. Choose to be messy. Choose sentences of Faulknerian proportions. Choose an indirect route. Choose something new. And open your ears, and open your mouth.

Without a significant change in the method by which we create work, Joe Client will, in time, catch up. Software is becoming more accessible, awareness is high — marketing departments already proclaim to know how to do our jobs — without a significant revolution, design as we know it will perish.

The ball rests motionless in our court.

Smash it.

1. *Emigre #6*, RANT, Denise Gonzales Crisp, "Visitations," pp. 50–51, Princeton Architectural Press, 2003.
2. *Less is More*, Steven Heller, "Introduction," p. 8, North Light Books, 1999.
3. *Looking Closer 4: Critical Writings on Graphic Design*, Robert Fulford, "All Hail Mau the Magnificent," p. 250, Allworth Press, 2003.

Benjamin Hagon is a British graphic designer currently residing in Toronto, Canada, where it is very cold in winter.

DUMB IDEAS.

MR. KEEDY

DESIGN THEORY: IS IT BACK? Since the thrill of digital technology has become an agony of endless upgrades, dot com millionaires have come and gone, and everyone has a roadside stand on the information highway or has published a self-promotional SUV of a book, maybe now is a good time to think about what's going on.

Reading design theories from the past, you can't help but be struck by how many times the same issues are discussed. It is as though every generation has to have essentially the same conversation but in a new way. Web logs (blogs) are the new way that designers are having that conversation now. They range from Design Observer, which reads like the Op Ed pages of a design journal, to Speak Up, which reads like "Chicken Noodle Soup for the Designer's Soul." As one of the many sporadic "lurkers" of design blogs, I of course enjoy hearing what other designers have to say, but it comes at a cost. You must be willing to wade through a seemingly endless recitation of dumb ideas that have already been refuted long ago. The only thing more annoying than having your ideas ignored or forgotten by the next generation, is watching them make the same stupid mistakes you made. So as a kind of public service, I thought I would start a list of some of the most popular but dumb ideas in design. Ideas that are popular because they seem to provide an answer, but dumb because they're wrong.

Designers just talking to other designers and "preaching to the choir" is a waste of time.

Yeah, if only plumbers, acupuncturists, and nuclear physicists were allowed to talk about design, that would be soooo helpful. A similar cliché is that "a broader range of voices needs to be heard," as if there were some malevolent force at work silencing a multitude of insightful design critics and theorists. How they manage to do it now that any nitwit who can work a keyboard is free to opine on any and all topics on the web is a real mystery.

We need to have more designers talking about design honestly and intelligently without the usual self-promotion and moral posturing. There are about 150,000 designers in the U.S. alone; a couple of them are bound to have a few good ideas. Obviously you can always learn something from other disciplines, but are we unable to learn anything from each other?

Design theorists and lecturers should refrain from using big words and quoting academic intellectuals. It just serves to obfuscate (see what I mean) their ideas, alienate the audience, and cover for the fact that they don't really have any ideas of their own.

This is the anti-intellectual's lament. If you can't say something quickly and simply, then you can't expect a simpleton to understand it. There is no shortage of small worded, anecdotal, *Readers Digest*-style accounts of design in "these United States" as far as I can tell.

It's a big country and an even bigger world. Next time you find yourself assaulted by flagrant verbosity and misguided citations, turn the page or turn up your iPod. This too shall pass. Or get a dictionary, read some books, and take some classes, dumb ass. Or take the offending pontificator to school and teach them by your own concise yet intricately nuanced example.

Content is good, style is bad.

Don't get me started. This is a dumb idea that is deeply ingrained in design. I, of course, blame modernism, and am confident that we will get over this idiotic notion in this new century, as it has done entirely too much damage in the last. It was helpful in the beginning for modernists to make the point that making meaning is an important part of why we make things at all. But it's not the only reason we make things. Meaning and content are contextual any-way, so what exactly would a styleless context look like? Who said style has no meaning or content anyway? Everyone should read *The Substance of Style*, by Virginia Postrel, the best design theory book by a non-designer in years. It may help designers get over their style phobia: the first step is facing your fear and recognizing you have a problem – with style.

Designers should always try to do work that is experimental.

I don't even know what that word is supposed to mean in design anymore. It used to mean work that is provisional, not complete or refined; a work in progress that is created to test a hypothesis. A student effort. Something you do to test an idea or technique, not something you do to publish or show off. Not that there is anything wrong with a kind of gratuitous showing off, but you shouldn't try to justify it by calling it experimental. The idea that experimental work is complex or obtuse and cutting edge is really cornball. We should be much more critical of anything labeled experimental. After all, that is the point of an experiment: to see if it worked. Legitimately experimental work is part of the design process and goes on all the time, a process that most designers started in school, and many continue with. It's a means, not an end.

Mature designers often don't need to experiment very much anymore, as they know what they are after and are working on refining and improving their vision and craft. For the most part they keep their experiments to themselves and just show us the good stuff.

Designers should strive for timelessness.

Yes, it's still with us, and probably always will be, because dumb ideas are timeless. But we won't know for sure, of course, until the actual end of time. Maybe if designers stop using that word, they will have to use other words that have a sensible meaning, giving people the impression that designers are sensible people. A similar variant of the timeless malarkey is the equally dumb idea of "transparency" or zero degree design. It's like Santa Claus and democracy: it seems to work as long as we pretend to believe in it.

Designers should develop their own personal voice; originality and authenticity should be their goal.

This idea is so last-century. The assumption here is that personal voice, authenticity, and originality are all good things, which they often are, but just as often are not. Everyone has a personal voice but not everyone can sing. If you have an authentically bad personal voice, you should leave the singing to someone else. And there is no shortage of stupid original ideas. It still makes for good advertizing copy, but originality doesn't count for much in design because design isn't very original. Design is about organizing and making, but not from scratch and always in context of use.

If someone designs an original typeface, for example, they don't invent new letters; they invent new shapes for letters that we understand only because they are so similar to the shapes of letters that already exist. It is not so much the originality of the particular shapes that are important, but rather the ingenuity of the letter forms in the context of all the other letter forms that existed before, and the meaning or significance they convey in that context. Uniqueness in and of itself is not very significant, nor is it as pervasive in design as we claim it is. Invention and imagination are very important to design but they don't come out of thin air, they come from the context they were created in, not from some self-taught genius.

Designers need to redefine their context.

The concept of context seems to have gone from something you are already a part of, to something you simply invent. Unfortunately, just because you say something doesn't mean it is true (even if it is on talk radio or a blog).

Context isn't something you make; it's something that is. You can have any idea about design you want, but that idea won't necessarily have any effect on design, because design is in the world – not in you. The idea of re-contextualizing design is like playing a game where you get to make up the rules as you go. You are only to be judged by your own criteria. And guess what? You win!

Design has become way too decontextualized as it is. How many times have you read a designer profile in which absolutely no other designer is mentioned other than the one under review? As if they were the only designer that ever designed anything and everything they say is accepted as gospel "straight from the horse's mouth." What's the point? Must everything be a self-promotion? Do we really get to invent our own relevance?

Designers should be more autonomous.

———

The idea here is that autonomy will give designers coherency through self-definition and a separation from the demands of the marketplace. This self-proclaimed autonomy is supposed to rally the troops because they get to make up their own job description. But an autonomous community is a bit of an oxymoron, isn't it? You can only get away with being autonomous as long as someone else is picking up the garbage and making sure the trains run on time. Sounds a lot like being an artist. At a time when designers can't even agree on what to call themselves, or what exactly it is that they do, it is not hard to see why an "every man for himself" attitude is popular. When I think of the autonomous designer, I imagine a self-taught ten year old with a laptop.

Design criticism and theory are just personal opinions, not facts.

Well, duh! But opinions and so-called facts are not mutually exclusive. Facts start as opinions first. If they pass muster, they become facts. Opinions are as valuable as facts in the development of knowledge. The sentiment above implies that one person's opinions are as valid as and equal to anyone else's. In spite of what you may have been told in kindergarten, or a lit. crit. class in grad school, that is (in fact) not true. However, uninformed opinions do serve to illustrate how not to think about something. That is why discernment and the critical process are important, why opinions are important, not just facts (which should be contested from time to time as well).

People get good at what they do by working at it. Discussing, studying, and writing are all part of the work that is essential to understand what constitutes the primary issues, values, and criteria of a discipline, and develop the strategies that move it forward. The dictionary says that an opinion is "a belief stronger than an impression and less strong than personal knowledge, and it is a formal statement by an expert after careful study." What's wrong with that?

Design theory is for making sense of design practice.

I think of theory as coming in three flavors: methodology, criticism, and "pure" theory. Methodology is probably the most directly related to practice because you first have to know "how to" practice. Criticism happens after the fact and is a bit more removed from practice by a "critical distance." And finally, "pure" theory may or may not be related to practice at all. Most design theory consists of a mix of these three flavors in various combinations and often has a bit of history, philosophy, and politics thrown in, as well.

When I first started teaching design theory at Otis Parsons in 1987, I put a lot of effort into making connections between theory and practice for the students, as if to justify the need for a theory class at all. By trying to "connect the dots" for them, I was teaching theory as a critical methodology for use in practice. Although critical and methodological thinking is really useful, probably the most useful thing a designer can get from theory is inspiration. But by insisting on direct and (often obvious) relevance to practice, theory becomes less useful as an idea because it loses its ability to inspire. I think that is why designers who insist that "design is about ideas" don't seem to ever have any. They think it is enough to be for the idea of having ideas. Who isn't? But they lack the inspiration to find them.

In the theory classes I teach at CalArts now, it is up to the students to "connect the dots" between theory, the studio, their own work, and the world. Tibor Kalman said "We need more why and less how." I think we need more why, how, and why not?

You can't separate form from content.

Yes, you can. You can separate form from its "original" content and attach it to a new content (pastiche), but it always retains some vestige of its "original" content. For example, Raymond Loewy's pencil sharpener looks like it is going to take flight, because its streamlined form was separated from the aerodynamics of air-planes. Things get even more complicated when you mix multiple forms and contents together (eclecticism). You can separate a form and content from each other, but you can't have content without form or form without content. Even though designers talk about "empty formalism," forms are never completely devoid of content, because forms come from somewhere, and they bring with them vestigial content.

Designers play in the space between form and content all the time, but they are pretty lax about articulating the subtlety and

complexity of the relationship between them, and words like
pastiche and eclecticism are too sweeping in scope to be much help.

What is needed in design is a new...

You can fill in the rest of the sentence with almost anything, and
it will probably still qualify as a dumb idea. Past favorites have been
new rules/context/wave/resistance/sobriety/complexity/autonomy/
paradigm for the new desktop/digital/interactive/web/motion/
virtual/corporate/cultural, whatever. Usually championed by someone who didn't really know much about the "old" whatever, other
than the fact that it desperately needs replacing.

I, for one, have certainly not been immune to the charms of
the new, and its pal "the next big thing." They are full of promise,
but seldom deliver. Try this little experiment: every time you read,
write, or say the word "new" in relation to design: replace it with
the word "good."

It is a lot easier to be new than it is to be good. The criteria for
being new is only based on the past few years, but the criteria for
being good is based on everything we have learned since the beginning of time. However, you actually have to know history before
you can use it as a criterion for judgment. By working "intuitively"
rather than intellectually, designers can convince themselves and
their clients that they are creating "new" work, and newness is
exactly what clients want to make boring products seem interesting.
In this respect designers are rewarded more for their ignorance
than for their insight. That's why many designers don't bother with
the past beyond what they have experienced themselves. When
was the last time you heard a designer bragging about doing the
"oldest" thing?

Designers enjoy being the arbiters of fashion and ignorance is
a small and easy price to pay for the privilege. The idea that "there

is nothing new under the sun" is an old one, but do we really have to insist that everything be new? It is a lot more likely that a useless piece of crap will be new than old, because the test of time tends to throw most of the crap out. I'm willing to settle for just good.

Mr. Keedy is a designer, writer, type designer, and educator who lives in Los Angeles.

AN INTERVIEW

WITH

DAVID CABIANCA.

———

DECEMBER 2003

THE FOLLOWING INTERVIEW with David Cabianca came about after I received his letter to the editor commenting on *Emigre* #64, RANT. I liked the content of his letter, but felt the language was too academic. This started a discussion about writing for design magazines, which grew into this interview. David's letter was published, in a slightly edited form, in *Emigre* #65 (P. 124).

Q | **Rudy VanderLans:** You mentioned that because your Cranbrook degree seems to scare off employers and academic institutions alike, you are currently attending the 12 month MA in Typeface Design at the University of Reading in the UK. First, what is it about Cranbrook that scares people? Second, what do you hope to take away from Reading that will better prepare you for either employers or the academic world?

A | **David Cabianca:** I chose to go to Cranbrook because I was teaching architecture at the University of Michigan and I found myself captivated by what was going on at Cranbrook. I recall attending a Studio Dumbar symposium at the Cranbrook Art Museum and Laurie and Scott Makela gave a visual and aural performance that still makes my spine tingle. That was my first experience of understanding what graphic design could offer. At the time, it was the closest thing I had come to in graphic design that yielded the same experience that architecture – when at its best – can convey.

During my two years under Laurie's direction, she would often say, "Experience before theory," which didn't mean that theory was the stepchild. Experience is the theory. Theory is not divorced from experience and applied artificially. The two are inseparable. Experience is a haptic thing; it is visceral and Laurie Makela wanted us to make work that made one feel theory in the gut, to make spines tingle.

This, coupled with a background in architecture, makes my work rather opaque and divorced from what I would call "conceptual illustration." I am drawn to artists (Viola, Serra), architects

(Herzog, de Meuron, Zumthor), and authors (Beckett, Fuentes) who have an idea or perspective about the world beyond an immediate message. Ad agencies in particular find my design work difficult to digest because there is no "quick read" or easily sellable message. I don't mean to speak for all my peers, but it may be fair to say that Cranbrook breeds work that requires some reflection.

Cranbrook certainly didn't leave me unprepared for practice or teaching. Besides having a razor-sharp mind, Laurie is an immensely talented designer who is able to channel her abilities into her teaching. But the perception from the design schools I met with was that even though my portfolio had a strong typographic base, because there are no classes at Cranbrook I couldn't possibly know enough to teach typography and graphic design history. They also couldn't see that having a Master of Architecture degree from Princeton might mean that I had the skills and abilities to produce a design curriculum. My choice to attend Reading is a response to that, but it is also a natural outgrowth of my background. Moving from architecture to type design is very natural for me: both are relatively structured, conceptually abstract, and formally non-figural. Reading may be at the other end of the design spectrum from Cranbrook, but its standards for quality and discourse are on par with my experiences at Princeton and Cranbrook.

Q | Do you think there is a future for design criticism?

A | Like the expression, "People read best what they read most," I think that people accept theory and criticism the more they are exposed to it. But it is not a matter of speaking about theory and criticism in some third person way, as though it were a pill to swallow. By "theory," I am referring to something very specific: at its best, theory is a way of thinking about the world. But it doesn't guarantee any outcome. For instance, there may not be a practical application for thinking about an idea in a particular way, but it may foster a sense of curiosity about the world.

Q | My experience is different. The more theory we publish in *Emigre*, the fewer people read *Emigre*. And I know it has a lot to do with the way the essays are written. The language is either too academic for most people, which makes their heads hurt, or at other times, the writing is just not very good; it doesn't engage, because not enough people dedicate their careers to writing. Most people do it alongside their teaching or professional design careers. It takes a lot of hard work to become a good writer. Your initial letter to *Emigre* had that overly academic tone, almost like an affectation (sorry to be so blunt).

A | I know I write in an academic manner, and I know that with practice I can learn to better temper my language. But I figure that when I am trying to come to terms with stuff I find difficult to read, I always think, "What do I need to do in order to better understand this material?" I never blame the author; I try to raise myself to the level of the material I am reading.

I found the recent exchange between Matt Soar and Paula Scher in *Eye*,[1] and Rick Poynor's analysis of the exchange in *Print*,[2] both fascinating and irritating. My biggest contention is the recurring call for "design educators to talk to ordinary designers in a way designers can understand. [Poynor]" First off, professional designers were once students, so I'm left to wonder what kind of education they had if they can no longer follow discourse after leaving the academy. This may seem a harsh or pompous comment, but I think that students should demand more from their programs. It is a disservice to an individual and to society when an education has been shortchanged. Secondly, there never seems to be a reciprocal call for design professionals to elevate their understanding and use of language. We are not speaking to clients here, but to other designers. No one faults a lawyer or a doctor for using very specific language when discussing their respective practices with other lawyers or doctors. In fact, if I needed to hire a lawyer, I would want one whose command of

language is particularly fine-tuned and precise, and similarly
I would want a doctor whose medical knowledge is steeped in
the jargon of his specialty.

Q | Yes, you'd want a doctor steeped in the jargon of his specialty, and
not one who's skilled in the language of medical criticism (if such
a thing exists). These are two different things. The question is,
can one benefit from the other?

A | No, I disagree. I am referring to an informed use of language that
reflects knowledge about one's craft (which may be writing about
graphic design or practicing it). Whether language is put to use
for a trial defense, cancer research, or scholarly discussion is
beside the point. The ability to express ideas verbally is as much a
reflection of skill and talent as the ability to express ideas visually.

To return to your question: yes, practice and criticism can
benefit from each other. Ultimately, both Matt Soar and Paula
Scher are right. Academia and practice function best when there
is a certain amount of friction between the two. Each challenges
and propels the other. It is irresponsible for either position to
state that the other is irrelevant. Without academia, practice is
reduced to a technical skill and without practice, academia is
reduced to an abstraction. The solution lies in the understanding
that there are different ways to practice graphic design. Some do
it through print, others through the web or the gallery system,
and still others do it through writing and criticism. I mean this in
all earnestness when I say that I am looking forward to the day
Rick Poynor can feel comfortable enough to introduce himself as
"Rick Poynor, Graphic Designer" at an AIGA conference.

Q | But this "academic" writing – the form, the incessant quoting and
referring, and rehashing of established insider ideas – will make
many people who could benefit from it tune out.

A | Maybe I can afford that luxury because I am not an editor, but actually I am not really concerned with the tuning out of a particular audience. I am not trying to make "converts" of anyone. I think if someone is intellectually engaged, they are going to be curious about what they are reading, and that's all I am asking for. I can only hope that the seeds of curiosity have been or might be planted. But I think this may be an uphill battle. I have lost count of the number of design graduates I have met who have never heard of *Emigre*! This makes no sense to me because by now the journal is something of an institution.

Q | Let me quote part of your letter to *Emigre*: "Generally speaking, one of the productivist aims of the historical avant-garde has been achieved: technology is infinitely available to society today. But at the same time, the dissemination of technology and the saturating effects of mass culture have eliminated disciplinary specificity and individual aesthetic experience." That's a very condensed idea, and I have a vague idea of what you mean. But what does "disciplinary specificity" really mean? This is perhaps a little naive to ask, but when you write a sentence like this, is it entirely crystal clear to you?

A | I hope so, since I am using those words. Princeton is perhaps an immersive language environment. Words are taken very seriously. I don't think that it is a coincidence that someone like Toni Morrison continues to teach there. Language is very much a part of the air. That being the case, I find writing extremely painful because I agonize over the choice of each word. Words reveal how we think about ourselves, others, and the world. I don't recall where I read it, but after the start of the current war with Iraq, someone did an interesting analysis on the American TV networks and what their on-air logo decided to call the war. The words each network chose for its logo said a lot about its politics.

To answer your question about "disciplinary specificity": Each discipline – painting, literature, law, medicine, et al – has specific ways to see the world. Each uses representative tactics that are specific to a body of knowledge that "initiates" (i.e., designers in our case) comprehend and employ. For example, graphic designers speak of typography and the merits of one cut of Garamond over another. Today, anyone with access to a Mac and Photoshop can set up shop as a designer. This means that a whole generation has in effect skipped the initiation process of learning design and can call themselves designers. (This doesn't prevent one from making quality work, but it does mean that an individual has to develop a critical attitude toward their own work elsewhere.)

The phrase "elimination of individual aesthetic experience" refers to the notion that we not only take for granted the presence of global media, but we are trained to react in the same way to the same situations and have come to expect this global experience as the norm. For example, I found it very odd to be to be a Canadian in Reading discussing past TV episodes of *Friends* with Greek and Finnish classmates. Yet when I pointed this out, my classmate didn't see anything peculiar about it. As graphic designers, we are conditioned to restrain ourselves from exploring our craft and expressing our visual interests in the service of the message. We are told that any hint of self-expression will interfere with the message of the client. So what we end up with is a homogenized visual environment and a homogenized experience of that environment.

Q | And that's why, as you write, "Self-expression serves a potentially critical purpose today." To which most designers will reply: "Nobody pays me to express myself or to be critical." How do you respond to that?

A | It's a matter of context. I realize that designers have to pay bills and put food on the table. I think this discussion has been about goals and standards in design. When I was teaching, I tried to instill a sense of quality, ethics, and desire to learn, among other things.

I could respond that no one pays me to write about work that I don't find interesting, but I have a problem with the *laissez faire* attitude.

Q | What is the purpose of design criticism? If the purpose is to expand or improve the profession of graphic design, doesn't it stand to reason that you will have to address those who actually practice design? or do you see the value and purpose of criticism to be something entirely different? Do you perhaps see design criticism as something that can exist separately from design? Something practicing designers can come and visit from time to time if they are so inclined, but won't lose out on anything if they never partake?

A | Criticism is a learned skill like using Illustrator or playing the piano, and both criticism and theory can exist parallel to practice. But this certainly does not mean that critics can lose sight of the craft of design. Practicing designers see the world in a particular way and likewise practicing writers see the world in their own way. We conventionally think of criticism as being there to improve the process of thought, and hopefully this leads to better design, but criticism is a two-way street and design can teach us about being critical as well. Paula Scher is someone who operates in this manner whether she may or may not acknowledge it.

I don't think it is necessary that a practitioner employ the language of criticism in order to embody a critical practice. But like critical writing, a critical practice must follow the same principles: it has a point of view, it is aware of context and history, and it is well executed.

Q | Can you give me an example of a graphic designer/studio that embodies a critical practice?

A | I can think of a number of individuals who make it a core function of their output, but I think it is also true that there are a lot more people doing so that I am not aware of. This may be dodging the question somewhat because I'm putting forward two Cranbrook alumni, but Elliott Earls and Andrew Blauvelt are two designers whose work I admire because it represents a consistent commitment. Both Elliott and Andrew produce work that makes us think harder about design in particular and culture in general.

Q | You wrote that "Graphic design writing needs to develop its own techniques, procedures, and venues for theorizing its place in the world." Could you be a little more specific about these techniques, procedures, and venues?

A | With the emergence of PhD programs in theory and criticism, graphic design theory becomes more professionalized and writing will in general improve. I single out theory and criticism as a particular category of scholarship because the methods, theories, and concepts they codify from other disciplines, such as art theory, philosophy, comparative literature, American studies, and gender studies, have yet to be tapped as part of graphic design discourse. Their discourse is distinct from the behavioral sciences, legibility studies and programming sciences that currently populate the design PhD scene.

The PhD has the effect of producing new forms of scholarship and research which in turn may affect the training of graphic designers. At the same time, this will help develop an audience for the ideas produced. After all, PhD graduates will need a place to teach and the students whom they encounter will emerge with a different perspective on scholarly thinking.

Q | Design, to many who are critical about the profession, seems stuck, as is design criticism. You brought up the point that in the 1960s architecture was in a similar situation – it was stagnant – and that it was architectural theory that challenged the *status quo* and helped re-evaluate and reinvigorate its own theoretical output. This is good for criticism, but did it do anything for architecture?

A | I think that I am misunderstood here. Theory did have an effect on practice in architecture. I am oversimplifying a lot of architecture history, but yes, there were a number of significant ideas that had people asking questions in the late 1960s. Linguistics, phenomenology, and in particular two books both published in 1966 — Aldo Rossi's *Architecture of the City* and Robert Venturi's *Complexity and Contradiction in Architecture* — had people questioning the role of architecture in society. These questions were not being asked by established practitioners but rather by the so-called "Young Turks." There was not a lot of building going on because the economy was fairly stagnant at the time and a number of very intelligent and talented people — practitioners, historians, and theorists — got together and started asking questions about how these disciplines external to architecture related to architecture. There was a genuine interest or curiosity in making connections and staking out new theoretical territory for architecture.

These discussions or "study groups" led to the establishment of the Institute for Architecture and Urban Studies and the publication *Oppositions*. The IAUS and *Oppositions* went on to have a significant impact on breeding a new generation of designers and theorists. The outpouring of discourse from the Institute helped lay the groundwork for a steady diet of realized and theoretical projects, journals, and books that architects and architecture students now accept as the norm. Further, the overall quality of architecture improved. The infusion of the humanities made architects realize that architecture is not a science but an art, and that people need environments that foster a sense of well-being, not faceless concrete or glass boxes. The most significant result was that practitioners and theorists worked as partners. They had a mutual respect for each other and realized that they were both talking about the same ideas but approaching them with different strengths and perspectives.

Q | Even if we see the value of rigorous theory and criticism, there are two forces that work against it. One, there are not enough people interested in reading it, and two, there are few if any magazines supporting it and making it interesting, monetarily, for people to devote time to. How do you resolve this?

A | This goes back to planting the seeds of curiosity among future designers. I said in my letter that institutions tend to reproduce themselves and this is the biggest obstacle to change. I was told by one chair at a school where I was interviewed that I would be a great addition to their faculty if only they had a graduate program; they just didn't have room for a theory and criticism course in their curriculum. At this point I start to wonder whether the students graduating were attending a university or a vocational college. Students do need their technical skills in order to find work after graduating, but it is also important that they are given the ability to make intelligent life choices as well. This may be old fashioned, but an undergraduate education that respects the liberal arts is fundamental in my opinion. We can't predict the direction of the profession or the career choices of students and it is important to give students skills to think creatively and critically in addition to the skills necessary for practice.

Q | Perhaps there is a different role for design criticism; one that is aimed at others – design educators?

A | I think that this is bound to happen. But it doesn't mean that criticism is irrelevant. It has already happened in the discipline of architecture. As architecture students at Princeton, we often found that guest lecturers spoke at such an elevated level that it was difficult to follow the argument and it seemed that they were speaking more to the faculty and PhD students than the general audience. This had two effects. We learned that the speakers and faculty were at a level that we wanted to be, and we learned that we had to work hard to get there. We didn't dismiss the speakers for their language. We understood that ideas mattered and that we could access those ideas if we wanted to and worked hard, and of course we did.

Q | Let's change the subject here a bit. You wrote in your letter: "...authorship and self-expression...serve a potentially critical purpose today: authorship, or design signature, is a way for contemporary practices to imbue a work with quality." I agree with that. You then wrote "The irony of confusing a design signature with intellectually devoid formalism is to mistakenly dismiss image for a lack of content." I agree with that, too. But when a particular designer's self-expression becomes a mannerism used by all, isn't it fair to then dismiss that work as intellectually devoid formalism? This is what I, and many of the writers in *Emigre* #64 were getting at. Like you, we are interested in "probing the meaning behind such choices."

A | And this doesn't happen in other creative fields? And whose work are we specifically talking about? Of course designers are going to be influenced by others, and some are going to think, "Hey, I can crib that aesthetic, and won't it be great?" But a design signature is earned; it doesn't just happen overnight. It is more productive to focus on the originator than the derivatives.

Q | I probably didn't make myself clear. I agree with you that "Authorship and self-expression...serve a potentially critical purpose," and of course they are things that are earned through exploration and critical thinking. I don't dispute this at all. The problem is that there are not enough designers who dare to design critically. Most designers simply copy (to put it simplistically). It's these designers and their work that much of *Emigre* #64's criticism was leveled at. This endless repeating of mannerisms and stylistic gestures that we see all around us for no specific reason other than the fact that they look cool.

A | There isn't a positive culture of self-expression in graphic design. Instead, a suspicion of self-expression begins in design schools. Looking at the design work of others does happen in architecture schools and explicit references are frowned upon, but there is also a conscious attempt to come to terms with precedent and invention. It means analyzing the creative output of designers and asking what their work represented about culture and what impact their output has had. It means approaching expression from a slightly different perspective because architecture students are asked to make something new out of a conceptual understanding of the work of others, to "make it their own." This is where theory and criticism come into play. The culture that elevated David Carson in the 1990s isn't the same anymore, so a graphic design student may be asked to explore the significance of that difference in a seminar paper. This also goes back to the *Emigre #64*'s attempt to admonish contemporary designers for their use of a modernist design vocabulary because they supposedly are not subscribing to the tenets of modernism. Of course they aren't. The historical avant-garde never had the computer, the web, or TV. So there must be something else afoot that stimulates contemporary work.

I was motivated to write my initial letter because I found a lot of *Emigre #64* to be the written equivalent of intellectually devoid formalism. Criticism was applied in the abstract. Graphic design was treated en masse as something that that didn't seem to have a context. A lot of the kind of criticism found in *Emigre #64* is actually very easy to create because once they are established, generalities are easy to dismiss. It is much harder to probe the meaning behind specific moments in culture.

Q | If I understand you correctly, you are saying that most design is the result of specific moments in culture, and therefore we should look at culture for answers as to why design looks a specific way.

But that's just one way of looking at graphic design. Isn't it fair, and even instructive, to ask the designers what their motivations are, and what they mean by the specific gestures and styles they employ, particularly when they borrow them?

A | Of course one can ask designers about their thoughts on their work, but I often find that designers make poor speakers. This happens in architecture, as well. It is actually very rare that you will find an architect who is as good a speaker as he or she is a designer. Le Corbusier's ability to write well is what contributed to his appeal in his time, and is what contributes to Rem Koolhaas's fame today. The hand and the mind are two equal but often divided partners. I already mentioned that criticism and theory can exist parallel to design practice and some of the most interesting graphic design work is yet to be done by a new generation of graphic designers who are writers.

And rather than "style," I prefer to talk about "expression." Heidegger points out that we are "born into the world." This means that language comes with (cultural, philosophical, political, etc.) baggage already attached before our birth. Of course we can't get around the style/expression dichotomy, but "style" has formal, visual attachments that block further discussion. If I use the word "expression," people are going to want to know exactly what is being expressed, and we can move on from there.

Q | What is the value to design of design blogs? Are there any you read?
A | I think that there are some very good blogs out there. I think that design blogs have a very important place today. They store information that otherwise would be unavailable because their market is too small for other forms of media circulation. I'm a regular reader of Typographi.ca for news, Typophile.com for specific type information, Typotheque.com for general content, and, for obvious reasons, Cranbrookdesign.com which is run by two former classmates, Arjen Noordeman and Maya Drozdz.

A | What do you think about the current state of graphic design? Is it living up to its potential?

Q | I think that graphic design is extremely resilient. Some of the work I currently find interesting is being done by people who are fusing Western and non-Western cultures: Eric Cruz's "Nike Presto" campaigns at Wieden and Kennedy Japan; Alan Dye and Weston Bingham's work at Ogilvy and Mather's Brand Integration Group New York; and CalArts graduate Helena Fruehauf come to mind. I think these designers are doing some very fresh work that reinvigorates how we look at things in the West. And because I think they are doing some very intelligent work that explores the construction processes of ink, the fold, the bind, and the score, I also admire the work of Alice Chung and Karen Hsu at Omnivore.

1. Review of Paula Scher's *Make it Bigger*, *Eye*, 2003. Response to Matt Soar, *Eye*, 2003.
2. Analysis of the exchange, *Print*, "Up the Academy," p. 38, July/August, 2003.

THREE WISHES:

A GRAPHIC DESIGN SPEW CYCLE
IN THE NEW (AND SCARY) GEORGE W. ERA.

————

ERIC HEIMAN

1. *Let's get over this inferiority-to-artists complex.*

Last week I attended the local AIGA lecture by Golan Levin, who (according to the promotional copy) "develops artifacts and events that explore supple new modes of reactive expression." Golan's work, from a spectacle point of view, was quite impressive. Who wouldn't be seduced by cellular phone symphonies, computer programs that log the amount of instances a certain number appears on the Alta Vista search engine, and goggles that reveal color "blobs" that come out of people's heads every time they make a vocal sound? Then again, what does this work have to offer other than spectacle? As a former student wrote to me after the lecture, "[Golan's work] was very inspiring and engaging in a *Brave New World* kind of way. It made me wonder, though: How many answers can we really find in technology, and how [can] we transform experiments into design [that forwards] positive social change?"

A friend of mine, Andrew Milmoe of EAR studio, who was in town last week for the lecture, also creates work that occupies this fluid area where art, design, and technology crisscross. His most recent piece is a Pong game for the blind. It starts with a small table of 40 pennies arranged in a circle. Two crank-like "paddles," hinged in the center of the penny circle, are slid (or "swung") over the pennies, triggering an amplified sound from small metal arms that tap the bottom of the corresponding plastic cup on the 40-cup "chandelier" above. Instead of looking for a ball (as in normal Pong), they "listen" for it, and swing their "paddle" towards the oncoming sound to "hit" the "ball" back. Coincidentally, the local news this past Sunday featured a story on a local Easter egg hunt for blind children, using eggs that emanate sounds so the children could participate in a ritual previously off limits to them. These are examples of design that also just happen to be art.

Levin was a graphic designer at one point and maybe he's better off creating his idiosyncratic media art now, but I rue the trend of graphic design simply acting as a stepladder for talented people who feel only the label of "artist" will do, leaving that (sigh) lesser design to the rest of us. Golan Levin's work is design-based, but strives awfully hard to be art. Nobody likes the kid who is always trying too hard to be part of the In Crowd, so is it any wonder the art world doesn't like us? We come off as dilettantes. So maybe we should try to be designers when we design. It doesn't make the work any less valid (or less fun), and we may finally get out from under art's thumb in our minds and the minds of those outside of design, to forge our own unique practice that isn't just advertising, and only incidentally, not self-consciously, results in art. We need people as smart and inventive as Levin using their talents in the design world. How do we keep them?

2. *How about some new dialogue? I think we're in a rut!*

Last week, I received two publications in the mail: the new *Emigre*, subtitled RANT, and the new issue of the AIGA National publication, *Trace*. From all the emails I received from *Emigre* over the last few months trumpeting this RANT issue as an important treatise on the state of graphic design, I was expecting a jump start to the bad economy-induced lull in design discussion. Unfortunately, after reading this selection of essays, my response is "That's it?" After First Things First 2000, after 9/11, after an economic recession, after the VOICE 2 conference, after going to war, we're still just going to talk about *form* and *style*?

Mr. Keedy, in "Modernism 8.0" gives us a comparison of the first modernist style and the one being recycled today. I admire his tenacity on the issue only because I can't imagine caring this much about it in the context of today's world, design or otherwise. He might have used this comparison to push the importance of design history and context, or talked about how the return to a more minimal visual style might be about designers not wanting to bury their messages in illegibility and ambiguity. Instead, Keedy sounded as if this *nouveau* modernism was his next-door neighbor's dog that's keeping him up at night with its barking. Rick Valicenti's "Cranky" provides a nearly incoherent rant that supplies some additional id-based rage, but not much more. Shawn Wolfe serves up a more coherent spew than Valicenti, but his talk of the redesign for the packaging of Doublemint gum also feels slight, serving up only one good zinger at the end, "My passage to the past, to my personal past, is furnished with gum wrappers and old soda machines and 'brandcestors.' For me to fret about these facelifts is surely a sign of misplaced or displaced values." Even Jessica Helfand and William Drenttel, usually above such frivolities, only offer up "Wonders Revealed: Design and Faux Science," a by-the-book critique of the popular appropriation these days of scientific imagery. The excerpt from a dialogue between Denise Gonzales Crisp, Kali Nikitas, and Louise Sandhaus, "Visitations," begins to give some more depth to the form and style arguments, but it feels as if we missed the first third of their discussion, leaving more questions than potential answers. Andrew Blauvelt's "Towards Critical Autonomy or Can Graphic Design Save Itself?" does better than the previously mentioned articles, but spends too much time on a design history most *Emigre* readers would already be familiar with, and gets to the most compelling argument – experimental design vs. critical design – far too late in the piece and doesn't explore it in any depth.

Only the first essay, Kenneth Fitzgerald's "Quietude" draws any blood. Fitzgerald's piece does a good job of striking all the lightning rods in graphic design today, from addressing the lack of outside voices in design criticism, to insightful critiques of the deluge of recent vanity monographs, even putting a chink in Stefan Sagmeister's usually untarnished armor.

Ultimately though, RANT offers few solid ideas on where graphic design could go from here. *Emigre's* return to its critical format ends up being simply an extension of the frustration that most designers, educators, and scholars are currently experiencing, rather than illuminating possible paths they could follow.

I like to think of *Trace* as a switcheroo version of its last incarnation, the *AIGA Journal of Graphic Design*. Instead of the combination of some interesting articles and stately design, it is now featuring mostly historical or curatorial topics with an avant-garde design (courtesy of New York-based 2 x 4). This issue, subtitled "Postscript," predominantly refers to the tragic events of 9/11, but doesn't subvert the paradigm (9/11, despite its historical significance, is nearly a cliché now).

However, it does benefit from Rick Poynor and his article, "The Citizen Designer." You have to admire Poynor, if only because he's more dedicated to graphic design than most graphic designers. His essay is more thought provoking than anything in *Emigre*'s RANT. In this review of the AIGA VOICE 2 conference, Poynor gives the graphic design community no quarter despite the good intentions of the conference. He dismisses their fear of sounding or acting too politicized as if it would be too "off-putting," and demands more designers stand up and speak out. "The consumerist *status quo* pumps out a vast, overwhelming, massively resourced slurry of consciousness-shaping propaganda," Poynor writes, "What on earth is wrong in producing and taking support from some alternate points of view?" But in the next line, he stresses this will never be enough, and a Citizen Designer this does not make. No, it requires us to leave the safe confines of our computer screens, where we are in complete control, and venture out and engage with the world. Poynor continues, "Without such a level of self-belief (backed up by real ability) there is no way in which designers will ever exert fundamental influence. [But] essential to this...is a willingness to mix with civic leaders, appointed officials and volunteers."

Poynor then quotes Bennett Peji, a former president of the AIGA San Diego chapter, who puts in 20 hours a week running his business and 20 hours in voluntary work by serving on the boards of five local non-profit organizations. Peji says, "The key to truly affecting any group's design perspective is to effect change by serving on the board, not just being a *pro bono* vendor...Design is not the end goal. Design is simply a tool to help us connect to our communities and make a difference." Peji then talks about the results of his endeavors, which rallied a complacent design community, tripled its AIGA membership and gave support to city art programs at the service of disadvantaged neighborhoods. Poynor concludes by chiding designers for being too insular and urges those who wish to be architects of real change to find "strength in numbers" and "press design's case where it counts most – in places where power resides."

3. *Curiosity, Empathy, Humility.*

Jane Fulton Suri, a psychologist and head of the Human Factors division at IDEO, delivered the final lecture at the recent Graphic Design CONCEPT Symposium at the California College of Arts and Crafts (CCAC) based around modes of research. Most of the IDEO design team's research is based on observing people, but from the standpoint that the designers must expand their observations by letting the intended audience reveal possible solutions to them, as opposed to imposing their own preconceptions onto this same audience. The process is made of two facets: "empathy" – looking at human experience with a sympathetic eye to see what is truly needed by the audience – and "curiosity" – having an interest in the lives of the audience so as to further an understanding of what is needed in a product. One case study Suri presented was a design for a baby stroller. The IDEO team observed, first, that parents always seem to carry many accessories when they take their kids out for a jaunt; hence the final design incorporated more storage. More interestingly, they observed (through a technique called "shadow-ing") that in encounters between two or more adults with strollers, the children would often strain their necks to look up at the adults because they instinctively wanted to be part of the adults' conver-sation. So the design team made the stroller seat much higher than usual to help the child feel more a part of the interaction and pos-sibly less prone to tantrums. It seems apt that only a non-designer like Suri, whose focus is more on the audience's behavior and reaction to the end product rather than its physical beauty, could have come up with such a system. The formal characteristics of the IDEO projects, though beautifully realized, were secondary, if not incidental, to their function. This is a true illustration of design: an ideal combination of beauty and utility. Why has graphic design neglected the latter so much?

The design professor Paul J. Nini, in his "A Manifesto of Inclusivism," written in 2001 for AIGA Chicago's local *Inform* pub-lication, calls for a more "user-centered" approach to graphic design. He goes on to say, "While it's clear to us that the potential value graphic designers bring to communication can be great, shouldn't we perhaps agree that what we deem to be a 'successful' project must at least meet the basic needs of those for whom it was created? We routinely celebrate work in our profession's publications based mainly on how it looks. What if these competitions also required designers to demonstrate how they interacted with users or audience members, and how input from those groups helped shape communications that successfully met their needs? The results of such a collection of work might not necessarily look much different from what we see today, but one could argue that such criteria for inclusion might move us away from an emphasis solely on the aesthetic and at least acknowledge some sense of the functional."

Nini goes on to admit that all designers have experienced frustration working for organizations that they feel don't "support" their efforts, but also questions how graphic designers not engaging in user-based research can still honestly call their design "good."

"We ignore [the end user] at our peril and should take steps to allow their voice to be heard and address their needs in more significant ways," Nini writes, "We must attempt to move beyond our, at times, contemptuous view of users, and instead see them as collaborators or partners...For our profession to fully contribute to a democratic society, it must become as inclusive as possible."

There are currently some interesting examples of graphic design going above and beyond the usual line of duty. The AIGA, delivering on its using the Florida butterfly ballots as its *raison d'être* for the original VOICE conference, has helped establish Design for Democracy, an Illinois-based non-profit established to both study and implement improvements to voting materials, processes, and procedures nationwide. It's a team that includes, in addition to graphic designers, industrial designers, interface designers and specialists in anthropology and usability.

Another project was a collaboration between sociologist Patrick Ball and designer Matt Zimmerman. Ball, who specializes in human rights and social measurement, traveled to the Kosovo war region and interviewed thousands of refugees as they crossed the border about what had happened to them and why. Then he and Zimmerman created a series of informational diagrams to illustrate what was happening. During the World Court trial of former Serbian leader, Slobodan Milosevic, Ball offered his materials to the prosecution. Surprisingly, he was the only person in the world that had collected any real data about the refugees. Ball testified in court for four hours, and he and Zimmerman's work was some of the most effective, understandable, and damning evidence of the whole trial. As Nathan Shedroff continues in his text from *Adbusters* 44 about both projects, "While these solutions don't elevate their designers to celebrity status, they genuinely change the system and subvert the dominant paradigm — much more than, for comparison, MTV's 'Rock the Vote' campaign."

Not only are these projects elevating the role of graphic design, but they are also helping it get out of the commercial realm we so often love to hate, and hate to love. They also show that for graphic design to really matter, it has to go beyond protest art that is, more often than not, preachy and oversimplified (I, myself, am guilty as charged). Unique opportunities are out there, but are they sexy enough for us who have been weaned on the flashy series of *Typographics* books and designer monographs?

In my office, we are currently working on a collateral for the upcoming MONTEREY DESIGN CONFERENCE, put on by the American Institute of Architects California Council. The conference theme this year is "Doing Good, Doing Good" and this translates to a conference that is seeking to reconcile what we as creators consider doing good for ourselves (i.e., with this project I really subverted the dominant paradigm, I got a lot of positive responses from my peers, I built a great model for this project), and doing good for others, the world, etc. Normally we would start the process with some basic research involving gathering of materials related to the subject matter, and start sketching immediately. But with this project we decided to take Suri's talk to heart and see if we might involve the users in some way. Via email we sent out a survey to people in all walks of life, not just creative ones, that asked what the two "doing goods" were to them. The initial results were revealing in that they showed that most people, if not consciously acting, at least consider the idea of doing good for the external world in their work. More interesting, though, is that many of the surveyed expressed how much they wished to discuss and possibly get involved in "doing good," but had no forum in which do so. Sitting at home or in the studio or in the office alone, without the power and confidence a group gives, left them prone to do very little but ponder these notions.

We realized that this conference was one of those rare forums and our goal here was for the materials to do everything they could to foster dialogue between people. Our initial design ideas are to include these survey questions on both the poster and web registration forms and use them as content for the onsite materials such as the conference guide, badges, and screen graphics, plus provide interactive opportunities for attendees to continue the dialogue for all to access during the conference itself. This is all before we made a mark in our sketchbooks. Certainly this isn't earth shattering – and we will be providing the requisite "eye-candy" to give the conference an appealing, appropriate look – but to us this shows how these aforementioned methods can inform our everyday design practice.

This argument isn't a call for more professionalism, or an end to explorations of form and self-initiated projects. Obviously, we can't engage in intense research in every project. We don't always have the time or money, we like to be in control, we have our own opinions, and sometimes we just want to make cool things and play. We are human, after all. *Emigre* editor Rudy VanderLans, in his article, "The Next Big Thing" published in *Emigre* #39, says that the formal issues, so prevalent in the 90s, have run their course and maybe graphic designers should "Try [their] hand at judging design by its content, by the ideas and messages that it attempts to communicate ...picking [competition] winners based solely on the value of *what* they communicate, instead of *how* they communicate." After all the earth-shattering events of the last few years that have made us question our role as designers, shifting some of our work and thinking to a "user-centered" approach just may be one of the "next best things" that truly delivers on the concept of design beyond just making pretty pictures.

4. BONUS WISH *We should do it with, and for, the kids.*

———

The best place to percolate these ideas, of course, is in the classroom. Students are more idealistic and impressionable, teachers more free to try out new ideas than they would be as practitioners. The tradition has always been that new design theories should start in the academy and radiate out into the world from there. Contemporary design education's primary goal is to be as expansive as possible, without losing the center core, so to speak. In our work, we have to be (or at the very least, consult) anthropologists, scientists, psychologists, researchers, and politicians, just to name a few. Our field covers so many possible areas of study that we also need to be aware and consult our sister disciplines, such as industrial design, architecture, and art. This means providing instruction on subjects outside our normal graphic design scope, and it means encouraging collaboration with these other disciplines. If enough students come out of school with these expanded notions of what graphic design can be and do, the profession will undoubtedly change. Education needs to lead the charge in graphic design evolution, not wait on the profession to dictate the terms of what the ideal graphic design graduate is. Only then will we expand the public perception of graphic design as a solely service industry to a cultural and political force as well.

This is already happening. Bruce Mau and John Maeda, frustrated with the design education establishment's slow pace in evolving, are initiating their own graduate programs. This summer, John Bielenberg is starting Project M, a month-long design intensive inspired by the late Sam Mockbee's Rural Studio (where students design and build housing from reusable materials for the rural poor of Alabama) that will involve multiple instructors (including myself) in various disciplines encouraging students to "think wrong" and refocus their creative energies to solving non-commercial, more socially motivated problems. Both the graduate and undergraduate graphic design programs at CCAC (where I also teach) are also taking up the cause in the form of diverse student bodies, investigative studios, thesis projects, and new theory and history-based classes that are more expansive in their scope.

A quote from Terry Irwin in the May/June 2003 issue of *CA* magazine sums up our plight succinctly: "A significant perceptual shift is required of us — a shift in our perception of ourselves; a shift in our perception of design; and most importantly, a shift in the way we view the world. Such a shift could lead to new design method-ologies and more appropriate and responsible design solutions, and it is necessary to transition this profession and design education to the next level."

Eric Heiman is an Assistant Professor of Design at the California College of the Arts (CCA) and Co-Principal of Volume Design Inc. This paper was presented in April 2003 to the faculty and students at CCA in San Francisco.

VISITATIONS
REVISITED.

———

A REPLY

THE DISCUSSION PIECE "Visitations," which was published in *Emigre* #64, RANT, generated a large number of critiques. Since the published piece was an edited version of an informal three-way conversation (a rant of sorts), certain ideas were perhaps not represented completely enough, so we felt it was fair to give the authors an opportunity to clarify and respond to some of the criticism. Following is a brief interview with Kali Nikitas and a short reply by Louise Sandhaus. RVDL

Q | **Rudy VanderLans:** Quite a few people thought it was odd when you said: "And look at how few of the designers we visited were interested in what we were doing or what was happening in the U.S." You were being scolded for being pompous, aloof, self important... I'm guessing you were trying to get at something else. Care to clarify?

A | **Kali Nikitas:** My intention was never to sound pompous or arrogant. It was merely an observation, and I was expressing a desire to have more dialogue about similarities or differences between countries in practice and education. Funny that it took the publication of our conversation in *Emigre* #64 to get some heat into the discussion.

Q | All of you were described as not being "relevant" anymore, and hardly "current designers...more old-school academics," and that this is the reason why others in Europe are not interested in your work anymore. This comment intrigues me because it implies there are others out there who are relevant. At the risk of sending you even deeper into irrelevance, do you have any idea what and who is relevant in design today?

A | I am less interested in graphic design that is stylistically spectacular and limited in life span. I am more interested in how someone chooses to define their practice. In other words, what is "relevant" to me is someone's choices in practice and lifestyle and them trusting that the results of those choices will lead to great things.

Q | The entire *Emigre* #64, including your "Visitations" piece, was critiqued by many for being obsessed with style. In *Adbusters*, Dmitri Siegel wrote: "Formal novelty is not of urgent interest to many young designers...Young designers are focused on creating a context in which they can do work that is satisfying and new" and "this novelty need not be based on formal qualities." Instead, he writes, "The next phase of innovation and debate will be toward renovating the context of its practice." Therefore, discussing its form is rather useless. In other words, there's a sense that we're not getting it. Are we not getting it?

A | All young designers that I know are obsessed with form. And not only that, they are the first to critique form. What does it mean when it's said that they are "creating a context in which they can do work that is satisfying and new"? Does that mean they want to have their own studios and do their own work *sans* clients? Or does it mean that they want to start working in cross-disciplinary ways that redefine graphic design altogether? In either case, and I will say it again, *form matters*. Content is crucial. And content may drive form. But form is an integral part of the work, and to deny that is ridiculous and shortsighted. Even if it is possible to strip away personal style or character, the final form still conveys a message worth discussing. In some cases, that "stripping away" and denial of formal qualities is a knee jerk reaction to what has come before. It is a need for young designers to find a place in the design world that sets them apart. However, I would still talk about the work they produce in terms of *content*, as well as *form*.

Q | Recently you and Louise visited Europe again. You mentioned you had a different experience. Did you revisit some of the studios you met on your first trip? What was different?

A | For this trip we were only in Holland. And, yes, we revisited some of the same studios and visited some others. Quite honestly, I was a bit gun-shy after some of the reaction to the RANT issue.

It was very important for me to continue building relationships with these designers and not be seen as the American who barged in, gathered information, and ran back to the States bitching about what I did and did not see.

Personally, I was experiencing great disappointment in the profession at the time of my second trip. I came very close to quitting design and opening some flower shop anywhere in the world and living a life far away from graphic design. Surprisingly, the trip was really invigorating. I came home hopeful and happy. I can't put my finger on how or why. Maybe it had to do with coming to some conclusions about what I wanted from this profession and what I needed to do to find happiness again. Finding some of those answers made the trip worth its weight in gold.

Reply by Louise Sandhaus

After getting a gander at the various responses to the "Visitations" rant appearing on blogs such as DesignObserver and Speak Up, as well as in the publication *Adbusters*, this potentially cranky old gal of the possibly-has-been generation would like to offer a few reflections and clarifications, particularly about "style" and "context" — the heavy hitters of that conversation.

First, to clarify the purpose of my travels (physically and psychically) to Holland and London (places I've visited regularly since late '94). I was trying to seek out ideas that might stir the pot during conversations at CalArts and in my own practice, as we/I consider where graphic design might be going and where we might want to take it. Graphic design is a growing, living, changing discipline that is shaped by and responds to shifting social, technological, and economic contexts. I was out to garner some insights on those conditions and the responses to them through work being produced.

Part of what surfaced was that postmodernism, and by association work that might be seen as formally exuberant, seems to be the "current generation's" whipping boy. It seems to have been reduced to and relegated to history as a movement of "graphic free-for-all" and "personal expression and experimentation" – a representation that shrinks a significant cultural change to a vacuous visual style.

Postmodernism was the liberating social force after graphic design had lost its connection to context, and visual form had been reduced to reflecting universality, simplicity, conformity, and the illusion of global economic and social stability. Postmodernism was the impetus behind the upheaval of values that had become detached from the reality of the times. That we consider context in the first place – the very thing that allows for graphic design to evolve – is what this "movement," now reduced to a has-been style, allowed. The baby has been mistaken for the bathwater.

This misunderstanding might also be at the root of the complexities in discussing the value of visual form. If visual form has become equated with stylization and graphic novelty, no wonder it's receiving so much hate mail. As *graphic* designers, we create the means through which ideas are seen, experienced, and understood (for better or worse). I don't know what stuff should look like. I only know that to ignore visual form is to concede that what we do doesn't matter; that the visual is not important and is not capable of the kind of manifestation of intelligence attributed to words. Not to mention the means of engagement that words have.

POSTMODERN
POSTMORTEM.

———

SAM POTTS

———

First of two essays in response to the publication of Rick Poynor's book
No More Rules: Graphic Design and Postmodernism,
YALE UNIVERSITY PRESS, NEW HAVEN, CT, 2003

AS I BEGIN TO WRITE THIS REVIEW, the Modern Language Association national conference is just getting under way. The annual MLA meeting used to elicit an annual sarcastic article from *The New York Times*, usually the in the Styles section or the Magazine, making fun of esoteric academic presentations on pop culture and of academics for wearing orange pants. Recently, with the publication of Terry Eagleton's *After Theory*, the *Boston Globe* quoted Eagleton saying, "The golden age of theory is long past... [Theory] has actually been dead for quite a while; but we've been sort of behaving as though it isn't."[1] That didn't take long.

And as if on cue to mark the end of the theoretical era in graphic design, we have Rick Poynor's new book, *No More Rules: Graphic Design and Postmodernism*, come to draw some kind of chalk outline around all that crazy pomo stuff that freaked everyone out back in the 80s.

More a survey of individual works and stylistic attributes than a critical accounting of postmodern theory and/of/in design, *No More Rules* is useful and perhaps necessary to designers looking to orient certain types of experimental work in the scheme of recent design history. Although *No More Rules* is not a highly theoretical treatment (read: it's readable) of either design or postmodernism, what theory Poynor does introduce is done clearly and relatively briefly, sketching the general concepts of the postmodern period thematically by chapter and, more specifically, through the work of specific designers from the early 80s to the late 90s.

Readers comfortable with a term like "metanarrative" and who get excited by the linguistic hedging and layers of ambiguity going on in a sentence such as "As the 1980s unfolded, designers began to apply postmodern theory to a more self-conscious deconstruction of design's inbuilt assumptions and of its persuasive power as public communication" (P. 37) might find themselves disappointed by *No More Rules*, primarily because we want more of elaboration on what this sentence could possibly mean. A phrase like "a more self-conscious deconstruction of design's inbuilt assumptions," for example, should not be an encapsulation of postmodernist design, but rather the beginning point of Poynor's analysis. Such a phrase should not go, in other words, undeconstructed. There is a lot of ground covered in *No More Rules*, but a lot is left hanging, particularly at the intersection of theory-inspired work and a theoretical reading of such work.

Poynor writes with clarity and an expository directness that is at times almost a little too direct and literal for the characteristic inbuilt pliability of postmodern theoretical language (which that was certainly not an example of). It is always gratifying to find a thesis stated so clearly, as Poynor does in the Introduction: "*No More Rules'* central argument is that one of the most significant developments in graphic design, during the last two decades, has been designers' overt challenges to the conventions or rules that were once widely regarded as constituting good practice." (P. 12) Each of the books' five chapters (plus the first chapter, "Origins," which sketches a bit of the pre-postmodern) illustrates a theme bearing on Poynor's central idea of rule-breaking: "Deconstruction," "Appropriation," "Techno" (short for technology, not the music), "Authorship," and "Opposition." As he moves through each theme in rough chronological order, Poynor gives a fair amount of space to describing the very works that are shown in full color around the text. Such explication is standard operating procedure for any criticism, of course, but Poynor usually details what the visually astute reader (probably his entire readership) can already perceive in the examples.

Poynor's central thesis, and the critique outlined by his five themes, do not get much sharper teeth than his statement above, nor are we treated to a very intense analysis of the themes of each chapter. By "intense," I mean lengthy, complex, playful, exhaustive, speculative – something beyond the descriptive and the chronological. Coming upon Poynor's thesis, for example, I eagerly braced for some juicy parsing of the differences between "rules" and "conventions." *Rules* are the more codified, external, and prescriptive form of control, whereas *conventions* are more a matter of internalized prejudgments and habitual practices. Rules are normative and homogenizing; conventions are likely to lead to somewhat varied styles from designer to designer. Missing from *No More Rules* is a more developed analysis of the nature of these two forces, an analysis that seems crucial to any interpretation of work intent on breaking the rules (or conventions).

Then there is the problematic phrase "good practice," and it's anybody's guess what that may mean. I'm not being facetious here, because the question of "good practice" is at the heart of what we might say is the postmodern problem in design and also kind of in general. That is to say, it's very postmodern to feel that no one can agree on what constitutes "good" anymore, or else that there are too many definitions of good – so many that they're really all just examples, not a definition. What makes one piece of design an overt challenge to good practice while another is merely bad design? (Poynor never raises this question and I think it's safe to assume that all the examples given in the book are intended as the former, but a lot of the work from the 80s and 90s makes one wonder.) The matter of what *does* constitute good practice is important in any era, but Poynor does not explore in great depth the ways of talking about design in order to gain a better understanding of the conditions in which the work is made and the forces that shape it.

Poynor does provide some brief account of the general characteristics of the postmodern condition: "As many cultural critics have noted, the products of postmodern culture tend to be distinguished by such characteristics as fragmentation, impurity of form, depthlessness, indeterminacy, intertextuality, pluralism, eclecticism and a return to the vernacular." (P. 12 again) This list, and another passage giving some typical dualities of postmodernity – inside/outside, mind/body, speech/writing, presence/absence, nature/

culture, form/meaning (P. 46) – could serve as a means of talking about design and framing some of the questions mentioned above. But here's the problem: The development of various ideas from literary theory and philosophy (from which all the above are taken) within a design application creates problems for designers on two key points: the adoption of verbal concepts to visual form and the experimental-to-commercial arc of style. These are certainly not the only two ways that theory-based design is problematic, but they are issues raised by the stylistic emphasis of *No More Rules*.

FIRST KEY POINT. Postmodern theory is willfully, elusively, and gloriously linguistic. The jargon has become something of a joke, but postmodern theory in its core works is theory by and about language and the function and intercession of language in all other realms. This is an important point because it means that the tool of theory is the same as the product of the act. Graphic design has a much different dynamic between means and result, and the evidence of the effort to stretch the scope of the two is essentially what fills the pages of *No More Rules*. When graphic designers began applying some of the points of postmodern theory, they had to schlep the main (and it turned out more tractable) ideas from the original linguistic discipline to their (designers') own visual one. In so doing, designers transposed verbal concepts into visual representations of verbal concepts. "Representations" is of course a hugely loaded term in postmodernism, so perhaps "visual enactments" is better (and at the same time much, much worse).

This transposition was done in ways that seem literal and at the same time kind of raw. For example, Poynor notes that Derrida's act of putting a word or idea *sous rature*, or "under erasure," by setting it with strikethrough turned on (Microsoft Word makes everyone a deconstructionist, alas) shows up in Jonathan Barnbrook's design for David Bowie's album, *Heathen* (P. 47). A statement *sous rature* in the context of a theoretical discourse is meant to express a presence and an absence, while the key idea is neither presence nor absence, but rather the impossibility of excluding either of the two. A struck-through lyric on an album cover is a poor suggestion of this supple, ironic, and radical way of speaking. And so on with fragmented images and words, blurry "hyperkinetic" stuff, electronic-looking fonts (from Microgramma to OCR-A to pixel fonts), acidy RGBish colors, and all the rest of the postmodern designer's vocabulary. And while Poynor does conclude that "graphic design's borrowing of the label of 'deconstruction' lacked focus and rigor," and while he does mention a more interpretive application of deconstruction to typography (Byrne and Witte, P. 49), he does not pursue an extended visual analysis of either the ways that the theory supports the design or the design embodies or misreads the theory, as the case may be. The postmodern period in design was so theory-spiked that such an analysis seems called for in exactly this kind of book, and I do wish Poynor had gone further, as this would have taken *No More Rules* from overview to a more critical examination.

Poynor, while remaining quite neutral in tone throughout the book, concludes, "A wider application of these [deconstructionist] theories in design seems unlikely, even now that deconstruction has run its course as a style" (P. 67) which again shows the tendency throughout the book to look at the work stylistically rather than theoretically.

SECOND KEY POINT. The structure of *No More Rules* and the examples it contains describe a kind of arc from underground work to academic/theoretical work to commercial work that comes to rest in the final chapter, "Opposition." This chapter deals with certain designers' (e.g., Friedman, Kalman, Barnbrook) efforts to raise a critique from within postmodern consumerist culture. In other words, how can designers buck (no pun intended) the system from within by deploying postmodernist graphic styles and, more significantly, maintain a skeptical postmodern stance toward consumerism while remaining financially solvent?

The arc of style from experimental to commercial has seemingly become the inevitable fate of radically motivated design (read: theory-inspired design). As Poynor writes, "The problem [of developing a contemporary graphic language] goes to the heart of the purpose and meaning of graphic design...design's purpose is to help businesses sell things." (P. 171) (It's probably beside the point whether such a bald claim is tenable after 170 pages of postmodern design whose collective goal is essentially to refuse dogmatic statements exactly like this one.)

Because design operates in simultaneous contexts as a creative practice in the service of commercial purposes, any efforts toward the High (theory-informed, academic, "design with ideas") eventually reappear as forms in the Low (mainstream design, or as David Foster Wallace describes it, "the sort of art that has to please people in order to get their money"[2]). The problem for theory-based design, then, becomes: Just what *is* the purpose of theory in High, experimental design, if it's to be something other than a testing ground for the mainstream? If postmodernist theory helped designers to expand creative boundaries and challenge old notions of quality (and just about everything else), what is to be done with these new forms and this wider definition of what constitutes "good practice"? Isn't it more than a little disappointing if in the end the whole great project of postmodern design ends up just another *style*? Poynor's emphasis on postmodernism as a style neglects what may be the real contribution of this era: that design can become a more self-aware and self-critical practice.

In the end, there really *is* a need for experimental design outside of the mainstream. Such work should indicate the opportunity for all designers, experimental or not, to look critically at what happens when the experimental enters the mainstream, and in particular how designers can better understand and control this process. It's not enough to say that mainstream co-option or selling out is a function of a "complicitous relationship with postmodern consumerist culture" (of course it is, practically by definition) and ask, as Poynor does, "Where should designers who wish to engage in a rule-breaking postmodernism of resistance position themselves?" (both P. 171) This is because, I suspect, cultural transformation (Poynor's term) and the creative progress that could come with it may *not* be matters of design and style at all.

Common to nearly all the designers represented in *No More Rules* is that they are polemical within their work. Design that looks like it is saying something about design itself is postmodern design, and this is what we saw so much of in this period (not coincidentally in specialized contexts such as Cranbrook and *Emigre*). But this work now seems, upon review, to be polemical almost entirely about style and technique. The stylistic metanarrative in graphic design is internal to the profession — Poynor's original term "good practice" is a perfect (and completely vague) example of the way that designers are given beliefs about what's right. The real analysis of design needs to happen *higher up*, where design operates as part of a meta-narrative that involves economic and technological forces above and beyond stylistic concerns. At this level, who's designing your type-faces seems like a paltry concern compared to who's designing your software.

If design becomes a more self-conscious practice — and again, in the long run this may be the legacy of the postmodernist designers in *No More Rules* — the scope of design critique can be widened to questions of power in design practice: how the client-designer-audience relationship is a function of market and desire; how technology has democratized production (for better and for worse) at the same time that it has centralized control and economic viability to a handful of software companies; how design is both an impetus for and a symptom of contemporary cultural convictions. In other words, questions of how design *happens* in place of how design simply looks. Both the application of the postmodern critical method and the dual experimental/commercial role of design point to the opportunity for a wider critique. There is always a bigger picture. But design may not be a profession that wants to bite the hand that feeds it, or can.

HAVING SURVEYED THE POSTMODERN ERA in graphic design, we might expect Poynor to close *No More Rules* with some thoughts on whether we are now *beyond* postmodern problems and concerns, or whether today's designers are working on questions that belong to a kind of second-generation postmodernism (the death of theory notwithstanding). Such conslusions are not forthcoming, which leaves the reader at the end of *No More Rules* with more than a little feeling of indeterminacy, which in itself is very postmodern.

One of the strengths of *No More Rules*, despite its absences of analysis and reduction of complex questions, is that we do get a clear sense that postmodern design is all over the place. Form, process, technique, style — it's all polyglot and polymorphous and polymedia in the same way our contemporary world has been for quite some time. That sense, the sense of abundance to the point of saturation, is deep and pervasive and likely to be with us for a long time yet.

1. "The Self Critic" by Matthew Price, *Boston Globe*, 12/28/2003.
2. *A Supposedly Fun Thing I'll Never Do Again*, David Foster Wallace, "E Unibus Pluram; Television and U.S. Fiction," p. 37, Little Brown & Company, 1997.

Sam Potts is a graphic designer in New York.

CASTLES
MADE OF SAND.

——————

LORRAINE WILD

——————

Second of two essays in response to the publication of Rick Poynor's book
No More Rules: Graphic Design and Postmodernism,
YALE UNIVERSITY PRESS, NEW HAVEN, CT, 2003

IN 1980, MY FRIEND BILL BONNELL, a very successful and
elegant designer of the American-Swiss persuasion, was working
as a consultant on a brochure about some sort of customer service
offered by IBM. At the time, all design work for the company had
to be approved by Paul Rand, who was also a consultant for IBM,
though "consultant" doesn't begin to describe the command that
Rand wielded over that organization and its designers, both in-
and out-of-house. Bonnell, like so many others at that moment,
was exilarated by the typographic moves of Weingart, Friedman,
Kunz, and also by the graphic designers of the Russian avant-garde
(who were inspiration to those Swiss revisionists, as well). There
was a big exhibition on the Russians in Washington, which was one
of the first times you could actually see the work that had only really
become available in publications a few years earlier,[1] and a lot of
young designers were excited by it.

So Bonnell, hardly a rebel but alive to all this, made the tiniest
formal move on his brochure — layering a plus sign, which was a
meaningful part of the text — with its own shadow in the center of
the brochure. The plus sign and its shadow (approved by his client,
since it functioned within a design that adhered to the IBM identity
guidelines) reverberated with a sprightly energy, with its allusion
to the "deep space" of an El Lissitzky composition and the Basel
revisionists.

Thousands of the brochures were printed, yet when Paul Rand
saw them, he angrily demanded that they be put in the trash (which
they were). Bill was told to do it over and scolded like a recalcitrant
school kid. I vividly remember Bill telling me this story, and how in-
credulously funny the whole thing seemed. On one hand, how could
a little old drop shadow damn a piece of print (and its designer) to
the garbage can?[2] On the other hand, how could a guy like Rand,
who knew so much about typography, be so brittle as to think that
the minimalized modernism of the 1970s was the ultimate, perfect-
ed form of visual communication, never to be altered in the least
little bit?

SOUNDS STUPID, DOESN'T IT? Well, if you think it sounds dumb now, can you imagine how stupid it all seemed if you were young back in the late 70s? Can you imagine a job interview where you were warned you would only be allowed to use four typefaces (with no idea of what the typefaces might be used to communicate)? Or how about being told in graduate school that correct typography consisted of using only one font with one weight change? This despite trips to the library to see great books of the past, many of them typographic mélanges that would cause any of your professors to drop dead. Or how every "good designer" you knew started projects with the mechanics of the grid, and concepts seemed to be something only advertisers worried about? Or what if you saw the daily evidence piled up around you that the world operated with thousands of visual codes, but somehow you would not be taken seriously if you used any of them other than the desiccated form that modernism had devolved into? Could you be forgiven, perhaps, for beginning to suspect that what you were being taught was not actually modernism at all, but habit? Or bizarre fraternity rituals? The similarity to frat hazing was alarming; if you did what you were told without questions, you would be let "in"; everything depended upon emulating the cool, older guys who had managed to convince everyone that they were in charge. If you asked questions, there were no sensible answers and you definitely risked rejection.

PERSONALLY, I DECIDED in the face of all that I had already experienced as a young designer with doubts to escape to graduate school, where I thought I could recuperate some sense of design as a process, with a history, an ethos, etc., etc. That's another story,[3] but while I was there, perusing the paltry literature of graphic design, I assumed that it would be minutes, just minutes, until the art history students I saw around me discovered graphic design.

After all, art historians had recently discovered photography, and in just a short while, a time certainly no longer than the years Rick

Poynor documents in *No More Rules*, a rich literature of historical and contemporary photography had appeared. And I'm not just talking about picture books, but books with ideas attached to the pictures: historical documentation, analyses of contemporary work, exhibitions, and diverse interpretations.

Sure, there was an element of careerism in this. If you were a young historian of the visual, would you rather (a) count the angels standing on the head of, say, the French Impressionist pin, or (b) wade into the relatively uncharted waters of the most basic and ubiquitous visual documentation? The perennial lack of jobs for PhDs only stoked my own little professional paranoia; i.e., before I knew it, thousands of historians who knew nothing about graphic design as I knew and loved it (no matter how screwed up it was) would be studying it, writing about it, and creating graphic design history, just as they had for photography. On one hand, what a relief: one less thing for us busy designers to worry about. On the other hand, the threat of the uninitiated commandeering the story was just too scary.

About as terrorizing, it turns out, as Y2K, and similarly ground-less. For reasons that are obviously complex, if not mystifying, the story of graphic design is still pretty much below the general academic radar. I would bet cash that there are still more college seminars on Madonna (or, pathetically, Britney) than there are on graphic design. Poynor himself admits in *No More Rules* that though (some) designers have used critical theory, cultural historians and theorists have still barely recognized the existence of graphic design. Not that there is a shortage of books on graphic design, but most of them are picture books of interest to practitioners only (not that these do not play an important role in the field, but still...). And now we have blogs, and we do not have to worry about anyone coming up with new or original ideas about graphic design, despite the self-proclaimed rebellion in so much of the current digital "conversation." No documentation, no footnotes, no idea that anyone, designer or not, has ever said anything about graphic design before, other than what has just scrolled by on whatever thread you are reading. Every day is a new day on the blogs.

So I cannot be anything but grateful for the publication of *No More Rules*. I do not think it is widely understood just how difficult it is to pull a book like this together: to gather the material, clear the rights, substantiate and present the story with any sort of confidence at all. Let's just say that it is part of the reason that the literature of graphic design is evolving so slowly. Rick Poynor is one of our heroes; not a graphic designer, but a self-described fellow traveler who, as the founding editor of *Eye*, re-established (and reinvented) an international approach to graphic design journalism that transcended the dog 'n' pony show-ghetto into which most magazines had devolved in the 80s.[4] He is also responsible for one of the most important compilations of new typography to document the work as it was happening: *Typography Now*, in 1991, and recently, *Obey the Giant*, a compilation of his own essays on graphic design that have become required reading in many design departments.

No More Rules IS ABOUT GRAPHIC DESIGN produced between 1980 and 2000. In his introduction, Poynor claims that it really isn't a history as such, but an explanation of a period marked by new images, ideas, arguments, experiments, and technologies driven by the influence of postmodernism. I'm not sure this distinction will register with many readers, since Poynor's book takes the familiar form of a survey. He provides a clear a definition of postmodernism as an ongoing cultural phenomenon (rather than a formal fad), and he describes fairly accurately the commonly overlooked (or denigrated) relationship between graphic design practice and postmodern theory. He wisely substitutes the usual cavalcade of geniuses with an exploration of the origins of the work, and then a set of themes: Appropriation, Techno, Authorship, and Opposition.

Poynor's selection of work for his survey is very specific: a narrow band of academic design work of all types (often not properly identified as student projects, not then, not now); some pop culture stuff (mostly record sleeves); some small-run magazines, posters, club flyers, and design used to speak to other designers, like AIGA announcements or paper promotions. Probably the most "mass-market" examples depicted are Benetton's *Colors* magazine, the *Wired* spreads, Brody's design for covers of *The Face* and *New Socialist*, and the infamous Swatch ad by Paula Scher.

Many of the original critics of the sort of work featured here excoriated it on the grounds that it was too marginal, not commercial enough, ultimately unimportant (and oh, yes, "ugly"). Of course, the very reason this work is worth reviewing is that it turned out to be massively influential beyond its tiny scale. The vitality of the experiments spoke to an audience that was ultimately seen as a market. That work and its proliferation, along with the shift to digital means, burst the bubble of the self-satisfied design scene I described earlier. But the reader of *No More Rules* would never know that from what is actually depicted, since the work is shown in isolation, without any sort of mapping of the way that the production and proliferation and consumption of the new work proceeded. There are no examples of what these designers were visually reacting to; no cause and equally, no effect.

And that's the problem with the book, to this reader who witnessed and participated in the scene. It's missing so much of the specific energy and texture, seriousness and rebellion, the orneriness and fun. As far as the late 80s and early 90s goes, it certainly is the only time I've ever witnessed designers arguing overtly about graphic design as if it meant something. If you read the LETTERS TO THE EDITOR of *Emigre* from those years, you begin to get the idea.

Another example is that people no longer accepted the blank judgments of design competitions. Jurors' comments were insisted upon, a new phenomenon at that point, believe it or not.[5]

POYNOR DESCRIBES A DIALOGUE published in *Print* in 1990 between Tibor Kalman and Joe Duffy that addressed the issue of stylistic appropriation. What he omits is that *Print* was trying to capture a public argument that had boiled over between the two at the 1989 AIGA conference in San Antonio, after Kalman accused Duffy (by name! on the main stage!) for making what he deemed phony work. Can you imagine two designers almost punching each other out over anything at an AIGA conference now? Tibor's attack, correct or not, was fueled by the same sort of crazy enthusiasm that the designers of the postmodern typographic experiments were running on. One could sense the end of a bad old system, and it was time to take it down, and/or reinvent it through a challenge to its visual language.

Since Poynor claims that he is not writing a history, I wish he had spoken to more people and written his book as reportage, because the story of the big generational change that ran alongside the technological one is going to be much harder to reconstruct, as time goes by, than the citation of theoretical influences. The reductive modernism that was advocated by a tough and powerful older generation was so insular that it offered very few openings or clues as to where design might go next (other than the emulation of where it had been). Younger designers desiring to explore other avenues were on their own. Poynor really focuses on the turn toward theory, but seems to miss that this was part, but not all, of a desperate search — which included design history and the investigation into vernacular — by young designers who had concluded that the only way to reinvigorate graphic design was to look beyond its conventional borders.

ONE OF THE PROBLEMS WITH the themes of *No More Rules* and Poynor's insistence that they all be viewed through the scrim of theory is that he imposes an artificial order where there really wasn't much. This results in the work seeming more programmed and way more dependent upon the influence of theory than it really was. Some work included thus seems anomalous, because it illustrates the author's theme, not because it is particularly representative of what a given designer did before or after the production of a given piece.[6] Poynor delivers his narrative without much of the backstory: I found myself wondering what the designers or their clients would have said they were up to in the process of making the work. I bet that Rick Poynor would be quick to point out that designers and clients are not always able to articulate their intentions very clearly, and he's right: those sorts of comments are to be taken with several grains of salt. But *No More Rules* is a "category killer," in that it will be years until someone attempts a book on the same period again, years where the particulars of motivation and ambition fade away.

Given all that Poynor has witnessed and documented (especially in the pages of *Eye*), I just don't believe his insistence that the graphic design he is describing was instigated entirely by designers obediently reading and translating theory. In fact, he does address the issue of the (sometimes creative) misunderstanding or misuse of theory, but by leaving so many other dimensions of the story out of his narrative, his concentration on theory as the primary engine of change misrepresents the impetus behind the work (and finally distorts our ability to "see" it). Without a fuller explanation of what was behind the formal experimentation, the admittedly challenging design and typography of this period can appear to be pedantic and/ or pretentious. I mean, who wants to see theory illustrated, anyway?

But — in the words of another genius of the postmodern 80s, Pee Wee Herman, "There's always a big but"[7] — the graphic design in *No More Rules* was simply not as purely bred by theory as Poynor describes. In the chapter on "Appropriation," Poynor connects the practice of visual quotation from either historical or vernacular sources with the critique (citing Frederick Jameson) that essentially says that when stylistic innovation is impossible, contemporary art (and by extension, design) becomes empty, and more about itself.

He describes the distinction between parody and pastiche (in a nut shell: parody meaningful/good, pastiche meaningless/bad). Then Poynor walks through his list: Barney Bubbles, Neville Brody, Tibor Kalman, Peter Saville, Paula Scher, Art Chantry, Charles Spencer Anderson, and on to Old Navy, describing their work as if it were created by a reaction to the existence of a theoretical debate (Old Navy?) around postmodernism, and as if "retro" were invented around 1978.

Reading "Appropriation" through the single (and simple) focus of postmodern theory therefore ignores the vivid, commercial pop cultural phenomena of visual eclecticism and stylistic quotation that existed as an alternate universe to young designers trained as modernists in the 1970s. The work of Push Pin Studios was so influential in the publication design world of New York, for instance, that by the mid to late 1960s, the cool modernist school of design associated with art director Alexey Brodovich and his successors was replaced, at least in the upscale mass market magazines of the time, like *New York* or *Ms.*, with rampant historicist typography. Not to mention the underground press; that was almost uniformly historicist as well.[8] It is important to recognize that that eclecticism was already a reaction to the hegemony of the photographic, typographic modernism established by the 50s generation of designers, such as Sutnar, Beall, Rand, Burtin, and Golden.[9]

In the 70s a graphic design student might be asked to study Jan Tschichold or the classical "Swiss" books of Emil Ruder and Joseph Muller-Brockmann, but he or she was also probably spending a lot of time flipping through the bins at the local record store, which were a whole alternative typographic education in themselves. It is easy to forget how full of nostalgia and "appropriation" the imagery of pop music was, even in the 60s (look at the typography of *Rolling Stone* to this day, which adheres to a love of the muscular advertising vernacular of the American Type Foundry circa 1920), or how detached and "ironic" the imagery of a lot of pop music already was, even before Peter Saville (though he was really great at it). Who can explain why those naked kids are clambering up rocks on the cover of Led Zeppelin's *Houses of the Holy*?[10]

Next to Poynor's theory books and the big pile of magazines and album covers I'm proposing, I'd add the ironic visuals of Warhol, Ruscha, Richard Hamilton, and pop and conceptual art of many kinds; comic books, especially the underground ones; psychedelia of all sorts; the D.I.Y. *ad-hocism* of the *Whole Earth Catalog* or Ant Farm's *Guerrilla Television* manuals; the playfulness of Letraset; the relative novelty of Xerox art and mail art; Monty Python; the deadpan vernacular of the *National Lampoon* parodies; not to mention all of the campiness of so much 60s culture, high and low. Poynor does mention the postmodern architects. There's no doubt that Venturi was important, and that by the 70s young graphic designers thought architecture was pretty interesting for its debates. And people were already scavenging through the flea markets for vintage clothing and old furniture and printed matter, too. The preferred era was the stuff just on the cusp of modernism, the 30s and the 40s, which was valued for its ironic contrast to the stripped down, bland version of modernism one was supposed to master.

And if you were a student at Cranbrook in the 70s, you already knew Ed Fella's "art design" (though he did not call it that yet), which was already anticipating the gale force of change. It was obvious. You did not need theory or Wolfgang Weingart to know which way the wind blew. And forward to the 80s: there was punk, the free-for-all of the Dutch work that was so inspiring (which Poynor does include), and where in the world is Tadanori Yokoo? I could go on and on; the point being that young designers in the 70s and 80s let life in to what was a closed visual system. Though Poynor translates this largely as a search for autonomy or self-expression, I strongly disagree that this is all that accounts for the energy and effort of that work. I think the desire to make work that participated with as much intelligence and vitality as the rest of the culture was what was at stake!

THAT CERTAINLY WAS WHAT MOTIVATED ME, along with so many other young educators later in the 80s, to begin to work by revising the way that design was taught; that, and using design history, understanding that the visual conventions of modernism were not timeless truths, but instead, the results of a visual response to social, economic, and technological change, and that we were facing a similar situation. My question back in 1991 was "If the audience has changed and the production has changed, and the messages might change, wouldn't common sense suggest that the notion of form might evolve too?" [11]

Poynor documents a lot of work that came out of the schools, but the limitations of his survey format hinder his explanation. For a time, some of the design schools were more responsible for creating a space where a little perspective and independence about the practice and the "profession" could occur than anywhere else. The formal investigations produced by students and teachers were produced against this context, which utilized, and was enabled by, a reading of critical theory, and had large targets. However, the forms themselves, despite the early resistance to them by an older guard, were so alluring (and so specific to a younger audience) that, like every other formal expression of a cultural idea in our consumer-based society, they entered into the life cycle of visual style; i.e., they were marketed. It was not only for the students' benefit that David Carson, for instance, regularly visited several graphic design programs in the early 90s. The designer who continues to make big claims for the mystical power of intuition certainly — and wisely — saw something worthwhile in the sort of surrogate graduate study that he could access through his travels.

ANOTHER WEIRD OMISSION FROM *No More Rules* is the impact of the digital tools for motion circa the mid 90s. There are no images of websites or frames of motion graphics included in the book at all! There is some discussion in the "Techno" section of the postmodern *simulacra* and the now charmingly old-fashioned optimism attached to it all in the pages of *Wired*, etc. But, again, Poynor's survey creates greater distinctions than actually existed between things that were in fact working simultaneously. Certainly the new "techno" tools had a big impact on "authorship" and this was expressed, again, through content, process, and form, since the space between conceptualization and designing (and publication) had so rearranged themselves as to make the functionalist paradigm of modernism useless.

IT IS THE INGESTION of experimental styles by the marketing world that seems to have condemned the designers of these experiments (as if anyone participating in the Western economic system could escape that fate) in the eyes of so many now, including Rick Poynor.[12] At the very end of his book, he reveals his contempt for graphic design and designers (heavily hinted at by Chip Kidd's pastiche of a cover) by dumping them into an impossible conundrum: that the "Purpose and meaning of graphic design...is to sell things" and that any possibility of design having meaning beyond this depressing shallowness is dependent upon "fundamental systemic change" but in the meantime, why not ponder "resistance?" "To what sustained uses, other than its familiar and largely unquestioned commercial uses, might graphic design be applied?"[13]

Well gosh, there's all sorts of work that designers do that falls somewhere in the spectrum between marketing and protest (*Emigre* magazine, for instance), and I would argue that some of it is critical to the existence of what culture we have, unless you cynically write off all culture within a capitalist society as simply serving a market.

THAT WE CAN EVEN TALK TODAY about corporate work, commissioned work, independent work, designers as authors, designers as entrepreneurs, or designers as socialist resistance fighters represents one small triumph of the "experiments" that Poynor describes; that design is not just one thing anymore, but many (maybe too many) things. Now we have the freedom to call ourselves designers or whatever, with no one acting as gatekeeper. It's true that there are "no more rules." Now you are to be judged on the quality of your work, period. Today the curious question is what constitutes the designer's mind, or the designer's process: but it's a collective problem, one that you see playing out in a lot of contemporary dialogue, even though it's a struggle to articulate. But the generational dissing so prevalent in, say, the recent responses to *Emigre* #64, RANT, reminds me of what it sounds like to hear young women denigrate feminism. They have forgotten that the very ability to "make choices" is the result of the work of their predecessors, and an unflattering caricature of the efforts of the earlier generation has somehow superseded reality. The design equivalent – and Poynor's narrative – is that all that postmodern graphic design was concerned with was supercilious theory play, or formal solipsism, and it all got used up to sell sweaters or shoes, so who cares? In "Context in Critique" Dmitri Siegel proposes that what "Graphic design needs is an opportunity for all sides in the Legibility Wars to come clean, a Truth and Reconciliation Commission of sorts. Then maybe we can move on and begin to examine graphic design as a process that inscribes economic and social context."[14] I wholeheartedly agree with Siegel: I just wish that *No More Rules* had supplied denser, richer, and more informed evidence of what transpired during the last 25 years, so that those who were not there to experience it firsthand might be able to make some sense of it. In the meantime, my paranoia about the historians taking over the story of graphic design has ebbed away; they'll never make sense of the tsunami of chat on the blogs, if it is even there to be found in the future, who knows. And every week, some undergraduate reveals to me that another chunk of the very recent past is floating out to sea, as well...

1   The catalogue for the exhibition *The Avant-Garde in Russia 1910 - 1930: New Perspectives* (shown at the Los Angeles County Museum of Art in the summer of 1980, then at the Hirshhorn Museum in Washington D.C. in the fall of the same year) states that it was the first major museum survey devoted to the Russian avant-garde in the U.S.

2   In a recent conversation, Bonnell pointed out that the typography of the brochure, in which he mixed Garamond with Univers, was also cited by Rand as an abomination.

3   For a partial account of my time at graduate school from 1980 to 1982, see "That was then and this is now: but what is next?" in *Emigre* #39, Summer 1996, pp. 18-33.

4   *Eye* made its debut in 1990; Rick Poynor was the editor for seven years, from issue #1 through issue #24.

5   See "Chairman's Essay" by Katherine McCoy, in the *Fourteenth Annual 100 Show, American Center for Design, Design Year in Review* (1992), pp. 4-6. In this essay, McCoy describes her idea to adjust the common competition format by encouraging the jurors to "curate" their choices as individuals (instead of trying to reach a consensus) and asking them to describe and defend their selections for publication in the Annual. Under the influence of post-modernism, McCoy felt no single idea at that moment could represent design practice, and opening up the jurying to specific personal choice (while asking the jury to justify their choices, for the record) would admit idiosyncratic and experimental works into the *Fourteenth Annual 100 Show* that might not have made it in under the old and unarticulated system. These reforms were also meant to deal with an old complaint against competitions as often presenting bland work because the closed nature of the consensual jurying made the choices seem capricious. Despite the greater transparency of the competition process that her reforms produced, the selections – and the reputations of the jury – still came under attack. See Michael Bierut's introduction "Planetarium," in *Planetarium: The 100 Show, The Fifteenth Annual of the American Center for Design, Design Year in Review* (1993), pp. 5-7. Bierut's attack engendered further debate over the "rules" and purposes of design competitions (which was published in *Statements*, the journal of the American Center of Design in the following year) but it is clear to this reader, looking back on it all, that Bierut's original attack on the results of the *Fourteenth Annual 100 Show* was as much about the inclusion of the sorts of postmodern graphic design work of which, at that point, Bierut did not approve, as it was about any qualms he had about the jurying of the *Fourteenth Annual 100 Show*. I offer this sketch of just one more of the many skirmishes over graphic design as evidence of the turmoil of the times (which is perhaps underrepresented in *No More Rules*).

6   The most glaring example of this is the *The Night Gallery* poster by Art Chantry (p. 86). The prolific Seattle designer Chantry has always been extremely catholic in his use of a variety of graphic styles, and while *The Night Gallery* poster of 1991 has the right date, Chantry's ironic use of many vernaculars pre-dates the "theorizing" of the vernacular that Poyner describes, and seems to connect Chantry to debates to which I doubt he paid attention. Following his discussion of Chantry, Poynor's description of Charles S. Anderson and his "bonehead" style seems to miss the deliberately anti-ironic (and completely anti-theoretical) nature of his work. So while Chantry and Anderson's work look similar, they are still bodies of work that are quite different in concept, despite their creators' shared indifference to theory (and despite the fact that their work looks good together on a page).

7 *Pee Wee's Big Adventure*, (1985).

8 For a discussion of eclecticism in publication design in the 1960s and 70s, see "1968 and After: Underground and Up Again" in *Modern Magazine Design* by William Owen, William C. Brown Publishers, Dubuque, Iowa, 1992, pp. 102-113.

9 Visual boredom and generational contrariness are under-acknowledged as motivators for formal mutation in graphic design. Two examples: years ago, while freelancing for Milton Glaser, I was telling him about some volunteer work that I was doing for the librarians at the Cooper-Hewitt Museum, to help them sort some studio archives that had been given to them by the heirs of Ladislav Sutnar. Glaser's response was to tell me how awful he thought Sutnar's work was; that it exemplified the kind of design (of the generation immediately preceding his) that he and his fellow young designers of Push Pin Studios were in direct reaction to. Edward Fella also describes his early Detroit fake-Art-Deco "shiny shoe" illustrative lettering work as a joke that he launched in response to the clean modern style that prevailed even in the advertising world of 1950s Detroit.

10 Apparently, not even the designer! Aubrey Powell (member of the British design group Hipgnosis, which were responsible for some of the most iconic and "detached" album covers of the 1970s), has said that when they were commissioned to design the sleeve for Led Zeppelin's *Houses of the Holy* (1973), they were given neither a title nor music as reference, so the designers just went ahead and based their design on a science fiction novel that they were enthusiastic about. (Pity that they did not base it on Barthes.) See www.superseventies.com/ac28housesoftheholy.html

11 Lorraine Wild, "Graphic Design: Lost and Found" in *The Edge of the Millennium: An International Critique of Architecture, Urban Planning, Product and Communication Design*, edited by Susan Yelavich, Cooper-Hewitt, National Museum of Design, Smithsonian Institution and Whitney Library of Design, New York, 1993, p. 202.

12 Even this is not a new argument. For instance, here is Sheila de Bretteville writing in 1973: "The rigid separation between work and leisure, attitudes and values, male and female – which, we noted above, is reinforced by the tradition of simplification in the mass media and it also operates in product and environmental design. A few new voices were raised in the sixties who appreciated, not only complexity and contradiction, but the value of participation in the popular vernacular. However, the connection and response to the multiplicity of human potential was lost as their attitude became style and fashion.[...]" from "Some Aspects of Design from a Woman Designer" first published in *Icographic* 6 (Croydon, England: 1973) reprinted in *Looking Closer 3: Classic Writings on Graphic Design*, edited by M. Bierut, J. Helfand, S. Heller, and R. Poynor, Allworth Press, New York, 1999, p. 245. In this passage, de Bretteville raises the possibility that it is impossible for any critique that is offered via form to retain its legibility once it has entered the inevitable life cycle of style.

13 *No More Rules*, p. 171.

14 Dmitri Siegel, "Context in Critique" *Adbusters*, September/October 2003 (archived at http://www.typotheque.com/articles/rant__reviewed.html).

———

Lorraine Wild is a designer, writer, and educator who lives in Los Angeles.

THE READERS RESPOND.

MAIL

Dear Emigre,
This email is a response to *Emigre #64*, which was my first issue.

I'm 22 and live in Brazil, where I have a lot of trouble finding work that I love. While in America and Europe they are wondering whatever happened to a once promising postmodern design (or whatever you may call it), here we are still fighting to validate it. And by "we," it's important to note that I mean very few people.

I hope you don't mind that I'm sending you some of my work. I love to write about graphic design, and love to discuss it as well. However, I don't feel comfortable about sending you samples of text. Not only because I don't think you would find anything new there, but also because our backgrounds are totally different, and thus lacking a common ground for discussion. The state of graphic design here is really sad and discouraging.

Anyway, I guess it would be nice for me to make an effort to at least try to write something about issue number 64. You and the others who contributed to it surely deserve it.

Maybe the promised visual revolution, which so many predicted and celebrated, never occurred because of a lack of necessity. A possibility doesn't necessarily have to become a fact. The formal freedom, the proof that non-function-alist design actually functions pretty well, and the apparent imminence of printed media's obsolescence really provided more than enough possibilities for the occurrence of, if not a revolution, at least a significant visual evolution. But as long as there wasn't a real necessity for such a thing (and it doesn't seem there was), you can have all the possibilities you want.

I could write a lot more about this and give coherent arguments to support what I'm saying, but it would be deadly boring, so I will just pass along to the rest of it.

The thing is, a real necessity is on the way. It will prove to be the result of what the digital-audio-video monoculture is doing to us (instead of "for" us). It is the lack of a solid conceptual foundation that affects a great number of other disciplines, not only graphic design.

The digital media only provide the final product of information, like the eight o'clock news or the math books that give us just the ready-to-apply formula. What the media don't provide is the information about how these final products were achieved. The result is deficient, empty instruction, and, consequently, proportionally deficient production: A vicious circle that leads nowhere but down.

This situation is creating the demand

for a counterattack. Although humans have reached a state of evolution never before imagined possible, they are still not happy getting home after work. Entire generations have fought for a free speech society, and now that this liberty exists in overwhelming quantities, nobody seems to have anything significant to say. The need for a new evolution, non-technological, is absolutely on the way.

Designers should be the protagonists of this evolution. But, for this to happen, we really need more critical writing. We need to get out of the common vicious circle of empty instruction/production. We need passionate writing. Angry, if possible. Well-dosed anger, allied to critical consciousness, drives consistent action. You did a nice job with number 64. I hope it strikes the right nerves.

Dado Queiroz

Dear Emigre,
I'm in the middle of reading *Emigre* #65 and already feel compelled to tap out this personal "manifesto."

Why do I need a manifesto? Well, in the world of professional design, I'm just starting out. I need rules, objectives, targets, technique and ideals to guide me through the initial learning experience. Frankly, without a personal manifesto I would be lost in the modern jungle of design. So here goes:

1. Avoid the unhappy and the unlucky. I'm not prepared to be infected by other graphic designers complaining about the state of modern design. These people draw misfortune to themselves. Nor should I help them – to do so may be to save the drowning man, but the result may be my own disaster.

2. Stick to the six rules of doing business that have guided me successfully for the last 15 years:

2.1 Help my client to be successful. Use a process for my work and deliver the same high standard, every time.

2.2 Explain to my clients why I'm doing what I'm doing. Do it in their language – not design-speak.

2.3 Ask the right questions of myself and my client: incisive, troubleshooting, expert, well researched. Then produce the right work for the client.

2.4 Be fast. Be systematic. Resolve design issues quickly. Do not procrastinate.

2.5 Provide design solutions first time. Kill the client's dissatisfaction with my work the first time.

2.6 Get ahead of the competition. What else does my client need? What will they be looking for in six months time? Keep in touch with other design works and critique the best.

3. Only listen to practiced authority and then ask questions of it. Avoid my peers and only look to the top five percent of designers and artists for guidance, advice, ideas. Avoid any kind of work, written or otherwise, from students of Cranbrook or any other academic institute; their work may be good but it must all be tempered with real world experience, client satisfaction and a general acceptance that the work is some of their best or some of the best of its time.

4. Only use words my mother would understand. Avoid overcomplicating the theory and practice of design. Avoid

tautology; that is, needless repetition of an idea, statement, or word.

5. Avoid discussing graphic design with my friends. At all costs avoid revealing my knowledge of typography, grid systems, color communication, and theory, rhythmic composition, picture space analysis, or area-to-line change techniques. Avoid discussing why certain graphic design works and some doesn't. Never say "Paul Rand" in front of my neighbor.

6. View each challenge as an opportunity. Twist each negative to its true positive form. Never say things like "superficial design = great paycheck," but rather "good design = good paycheck." Research trends, learn from them, utilize the best elements, and create something new, thus following trends in an educated and purposeful way. Picasso did this and so can I.

7. Create compelling spectacles and make them seem effortless. Utilize today's technology to its fullest and push it further. Demand more from the vendors; remain intolerant of bugs or "features." Deliver more to the audience with motion, sound, and dimension. Blend effort, experience, and inspiration to transform my work and make it better.

8. Avoid publications that pander to academia, snobbishly ignore the real world and appear both disdainful and arrogant. Avoid those that refuse to teach but rather take solace in pandering to mediocre designer mid-life crises. Avoid publications with contributions from American designers who visit Europe for two weeks to reacquaint themselves with European design, start and stop with one design house, then complain bitterly that no one asked them what they were doing. Subscribe to publications that *are* concerned with practicalities, *have* useful bearing, and with less theory and more example.

9. Learn how to draw. Learn how to handcraft letterforms. Learn that unless I know how to draw, I will always be insecure as a designer. Learn how to draw, then teach my children how to draw.

10. Improve my technical programming. Achieve expert status with the digital tool set I use everyday. Learn that I will always be insecure as a designer until I know my quadratic easing equations and understand the physics of motion graphics. Then teach my children how to program.

There!

I'm a new subscriber to *Emigre* and to be honest I find it disappointing and irrelevant. Or rather, I find the contributors irrelevant. This is not literature — it is a soapbox for insecure designers. Second-rate insecure designers.

If *Emigre* cannot pull itself out of this procrastinating misery of an excuse for a graphic design publication, then I'll be compelled to cancel my subscription. If you are going to challenge, question, and investigate, then please do it with contributors who are street-savvy and quite prepared to exhibit their own work for analysis. If *Emigre* is unable to accept changes in the graphic design movement and embrace them as opportunities for further growth, then I'm sticking with *Eye* magazine.

James Waite

Dear Emigre,

I've read *Emigre* #64, RANT, twice. When I first got the issue over spring, I thumbed through it only to be disappointed by its jaded voice. This was a myopic viewing, but needless to say, I put it aside and went to my most recent issues of *I.D.*, *Metropolis*, *CA*, and *Eye*. I found I was able to enjoy them while sitting on my sun-deck or toilet. My spirit was lifted and my mind was saved from any critical thought; I had just completed a hectic quarter of grad school and needed to unwind a bit.

Who needed "Literature for Graphic Designers?" RANT sat at the bottom of my summer reading pile, with its depressing tone protected by other books and manuscripts with a more joyful mood. I didn't have the energy to assimilate RANT's call-to-arms. Now, summer is over and a new school year is beginning. I must forge fresh ideas and produce visual work in preparation for thesis. I completed my summer reading, except for RANT. After returning the other titles to the library, I reread RANT from start to finish, and saw things in a different light.

RANT challenges the role of designers. Are we merely servants? Blauvelt's article calls this to mind near his closing arguments. When I entered the design work force over 10 years ago during my first undergraduate internship, my mentor told me, "Whether we like it or not, design is not about authority...or art or creativity. It's about service. You're giving people something they want. You're answering their needs." At the time, I could see her point. While service is only one part for

design to play in our society, it's the one most graduates will play after leaving school. It's the role I played because that's what I was taught to do by influential mentors/professors. Furthermore, I had student loans to pay off and a massive Visa bill looming over my head. I was at the mercy of circumstance, but had a skill set that could make me money during the booming 1990s.

When I left school with a BFA, I hit the ground running by producing logos, websites, stationery systems, animations, and annual reports. I was conscious of the bottom line for my own good and the client. I learned the hottest software just to snag a new job and paycheck – everybody wanted something done in Flash. Accommodation was the key to survival as a graphic designer and this gave me a feeling of success. On one occasion, I won a website bid solely on my ability to animate a client's logo. They had not even seen my portfolio, nor had I ever done a website.

Who cared? Design was my best friend. Forging my own style or stealing others' created new opportunities left and right. Paychecks were rolling in. But over time, I felt empty. I had no investment (other than time) in the work I was doing, nor was I mindful of any reason to take on a project besides financial gain. That emptiness drew me back to school. I craved self-reflection and what Blauvelt calls "inventive contextuality."

To say the least, I have been pushed to self-reflection during graduate school. I am questioning design, the role I play in its development, and my own practice. Maybe the biggest question looming in RANT is: "Where do we go from here?" With "we" being the discipline of design, I don't know that I can address something so massive. But I can reflect on how I got here and where I can go through inventive contextuality.

Inventive contextuality places value on not only the creative product but also what claim one has in its manifestation and effect. Such critical design – or critical practice – is being a conscious designer. It's about pushing the limits (to paraphrase a statement Blauvelt used from *Design Noir*). It's about self-analysis, questioning who or what you are responsible to and why you or your design has an impact on society, culture, or design at large.

After reading RANT critically, I realize that I have so many problems and questions in my own head, that I am hard-pressed to solve them for others. Why should I design? Should I design because it's a marketable trade? Should I design because I know how to use Photoshop and Illustrator? Should I design to solve problems for other people? I don't have the answers yet. And frankly, I like the questions better than answers. Questions pose challenges, answers yield complacency.

In nine months, I will leave behind the personal research and self-reflection of graduate school. I am confident that I will not be complacent. The days of mere servitude and problem solving are done; process, context, and ideology are of equal importance. I am confident that I will continue to question. There is more to design than the veneer of form.

Jason A. Tselentis

As always, we're curious to know what you think about *Emigre*. Send your comments to:
editor@emigre.com or mail a letter to Emigre, 1700 Shattuck Ave. #307, Berkeley, CA 94709, USA.

IN MEMORY OF

FRANK HEINE

1964–2003

Frank Heine was a designer's designer.
Besides producing such classic typefaces
as *Remedy*, *Dalliance*, and *Tribute*, Heine
was also an accomplished graphic
designer who, like few others, mastered
a wide range of approaches – from light-
hearted to classical, to modern and
experimental.
On the following pages we'd like to
share some of our most favorite pieces
from Heine's repertoire.
For a full overview of Frank Heine's
work, see the book *Frank Heine: Type &c.
Personal and Commercial Works 1988-2003*,
published by Gmeiner-Verlag, 2003.

ABOVE:
Page spread from *Tribute*
type specimen, 2003.

OPPOSITE PAGE, TOP TO BOTTOM:
Page from a New Year's mailing
for U.O.R.G., Heine's design
company, 1997.

Gift-decoration: designs used
for nitro prints, 2002.

Page spread from a self-
published book based on a text
by Luigi Malerba, 1991.

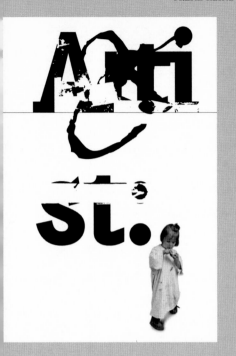

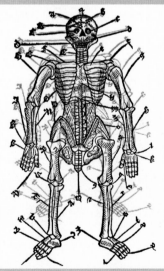

OpsmarcktBasic & Alternates   1234567890 ¹²³⁴⁵⁶⁷⁸⁹⁰/₁₂₃₄₅₆₇₈₉₀ $¢£¥ºⁿNº

Augustam Vindelicor., celeber=
rimam, et peruetustam, Superi=
oris Germaniæ vrbem, post funes=
tam, varianam cladem, subactis Va=
dalicis, Octauianus Aug: expugnat,
restaurat, auget, & tribus Roma=
nor. millib·habitadam tradit, Stra=
bo lib.4 · Hinc Augustj est nomen
sortita. Vngari, tum eam inuadut,
quibus ab Ottone I. graui prelio
fusis, Romano Jmperio, restitui=
tur. Sumptuosissimis ædificijs, pla=
teis amplis, ac nitidis, moenijs,
aggeribusq́ munitissimis, cele=
berrimis negotiorum commer=
tijs, polytiæ idea, incolis opulen=
tissimis, diligenti pauperum cura,
Episcopatu, &c. nobilitatur.

([{©®®@ ᵗʰᵉ&Q̄c.¶ſ*+=?!.,»"«œæÆḟbý́ỲàäâãâäøÒòŃÆ}])

Plus OpsmarcktBorders.   Design by Frank Heine.   Exclusively available from [T·26].

ABOVE:
Detail of an Internet site navigation;
a composite of Heine's *Amplifier* and
Mark Andresen's *Not Caslon*, 1998.

OPPOSITE PAGE:
Sample application of Heine's font
family *Opsmarckt* (and particularly
its border elelments), 1995.

BACH: BRANDENBURG CONCERTOS:

Wenn man unterscheiden darf zwischen der
Geschichte der Symphonie, der Fuge, der
Sonate oder anderer Gattungen, dann tritt
die "Geschichte des Instrumentalkonzerts"
hervor als eine der glänzendsten Entwick-
lungen der abendländischen Musik. Was in
der Mitte des 17. Jahrhunderts begann – als
italienische Komponisten in ihren Concerti
zum erstenmal in noch unbeholfener Archi-
tektur die soeben vollzogene Emanzipation der
virtuosen Solovioline dem primitiven Tutti der
Streicher gegenüberstellte, als sie diesen Wech-
sel stilisierten und zum Grundriß einer Form
machten – das endete in letzter Konsequenz in den
SoloKonzerten Schönbergs, Hindemiths, BartóKs
und StrawinsKys.

The CONCERTO principale has re-
mained constant in all periods from
the Baroque right through to that of
NEW MUSIC and has given rise, with
inexhaustible inventiveness, to all types
of scoring from the Classical concerto
for a single instrument to the many-
sided context of the BAROQUE CON-
CERTO for several instruments.
There was naturally instrumental music
previous to it (and of course after it
as well), but with the INSTRUMENTAL
CONCERTO the golden age of aristo-
cratic music, which raised the esteem
enjoyed by instruments and play-
ers to new artistic heights, came to an
end.

Dans cette trajectoire qui, déjà au XVIII.e siècle, produit
d'étonnants fruits, les SIX CONCERTOS BRANDEBOURGEOIS
de Jean-Sébastien Bach occupent une mystérieuse positi-
on-clef. MYSTÉRIEUSE, car cet ensemble de quelques concertos semble avoir dominé le développement FUTUR du
concerto instrumental, quoique, à l'époque où ils furent
créés, ils n'aient guère eu d'influence, voire de rayonne-
ment international. La cour de CÖTHEN, pour la quelle
Bach écrivit ces compositions, n'était qu'une minuscule.

Brandenburgische
Konzerte Nos. 1–6;
1721 dedicated to MARGRAVE
[Christian Ludwig]
von Brandenburg.

ABOVE:
Determination, experimental
type design for *Fuse*, London,
issue NO. 25, CITIES, 1995.

OPPOSITE PAGE:
Sample application of the font
family *Dalliance* designed for the
TDC2 competition, 2001.

EMPIRE

Nicholas Blechman, editor

APRIL 2004
7 X 10, 168 PAGES, 35 COLOR,
200 2-COLOR
PAPERBACK
$19.95 £14.99 €24 SFR 38

"Behold *Empire*: proof positive that when governments go bad, art gets good!" — Art Spiegelman

At a time of global crisis, *Empire* rallies a coalition of artists, designers, writers, and photographers to protest the mysterious, all-powerful phenomenon that dominates our civilization.

Featuring the best known and freshest unknown designers and cartoonists, *Empire* includes new work from Charles S. Anderson, Michael Bierut, Art Chantry, Seymour Chwast, Luba Lukova, Christoph Niemann, Stefan Sagmeister, Paul Sahre, and Ward Sutton.

ABRAM GAMES
His Life and Work

Naomi Games, Catherine Moriarty, June Rose

AVAILABLE
8 X 9, 208 PAGES, 180 COLOR,
70 B/W
HARDCOVER
$50.00
(AVAILABLE FROM PRINCETON
ARCHITECTURAL PRESS IN NORTH
AMERICA ONLY)

Over a remarkable career that spanned more than sixty years, Abram Games (1914-1996) was a leading voice in British graphic design. A modernist who used graphically charged symbols to catch the eye, he designed posters, signage, packaging and other ephemera for such giants as the BBC, Shell, British Airways, the Financial Times, Guinness, and the London Underground. His personal philosophy of "maximum meaning, minimum means" gave all his works a distinctive conceptual and visual integrity.

This first books to be published on Games features 180 color illustrations of his best-known works as well as examples of unpublished designs and sketches from his own extensive archive.

ART DECO BOOKBINDINGS
The Work of Pierre Legrain and Rose Adler

Yves Peyré and H. George Fletcher

MARCH 2004
7 X 9, 120 PAGES, 60 COLOR
HARDCOVER
$35.00 £25.00 €39.80 SFR 58

Before dust jackets wrapped every hardcover behind a shield of paper, a book's binding was its only advertisement, and the shelves of bibliophiles were lined with staid leather-bound tomes.

Then came the Art Deco designs of Pierre Legrain and Rose Adler, who transformed bookbinding into a medium of playful and dazzling experimentation and craftsmanship. Their colorful, imaginative works, often made in exotic materials, are found only rarely in a few prized collections and have rarely been available to the general public. Now, this selection of more than sixty designs, colored-paper maquettes, and realized bindings are collected in one exquisite volume, with insightful texts introducing the work and its revolutionary effect on modern design.

Among the brilliant array of bindings are ones made especially for works by Colette, Paul Verlaine, André Gide, Guillaume Apollinaire, Stéphane Mallarmé, Michel Leiris, and Jean Giraudoux.

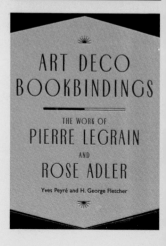

FRESH DIALOGUE FOUR
New Voices in Graphic Design

Veronique Vienne, editor

MAY 2004
8 X 9, 144 PAGES, 200 COLOR
PAPERBACK
$24.95, £16.99 €29.00 SFR 45

Fresh Dialogue Four brings together the work of three young and innovative graphic designers—Jason Fulford, Peter Buchanan-Smith, and Leanne Shapton—who have been selected as participants in the Fresh Dialogue series by the New York chapter of the AIGA. Taking the word "spine" as its theme, the book examines the worlds of publishing and self-publishing from the perspective of these graphic designers.

TYPE NOW
A Manifesto

Fred Smeijers

APRIL 2004
5.7 X 8.7, 144 PAGES,
16 PAGE COLOR INSERT
PAPERBACK
$27.50
(DISTRIBUTED BY PRINCETON
ARCHITECTURAL PRESS IN NORTH
AND SOUTH AMERICA ONLY)

Fred Smeijers
Type now

With the desktop revolution of the 1980s, typographic design came within the reach of anyone with a home computer. Since that time, we have seen a boom in the production of new fonts. This book takes stock of what was achieved during this protean period. Smeijers, a first-generation digital type designer, knows the possibilities of computer technology, but nevertheless argues for the continuing validity of the traditional skills of drawing and shape-making. He suggests that the trends of the recent past are already exhausted. As new industry standards are introduced, font-design must again become a job for engineers rather than self-trained designers. The book concludes that the number of new fonts being introduced must be reduced, and it ends with a proposal for a new "moral code" for type designers.

DESIGNING BOOKS
Practice and Theory

Jost Hochuli and Robin Kinross

MARCH 2004
6.7 X 8.9, 168 PAGES,
ILLUSTRATED THROUGHOUT
PAPERBACK
$30.00
(DISTRIBUTED BY PRINCETON
ARCHITECTURAL PRESS IN NORTH
AND SOUTH AMERICA ONLY)

Designing books
practice and theory
Jost Hochuli, Robin Kinross

Now available in paper, this newly revised and expanded classic in book design argues for a non-dogmatic approach, one open to both traditional and modern, and symmetrical and asymmetrical, solutions. A survey of Jost Hochuli's own work as a book designer featuring pages from a career of over 30 years is shown, along with detailed comments by noted designer and critic Robin Kinross.

"Hochuli has achieved his standing without any fuss, programme or manifesto, by sheer talent and persistence. This book is sure to help anyone who is seeking to develop a considered attitude towards the design and production of the book as a codex."

—*Logos*

Vendetta

This issue of *Emigre* was set in Vendetta, a family of eleven fonts designed circa 1997-99 by John Downer. Vendetta is licensed and distributed by Emigre Fonts and can be viewed and purchased at www.emigre.com.

VENDETTA MEDIUM

ABCDEFGHIJKLMNO
PQRSTUVWXYZ
abcdefghijklmnopqrstu
vwxyz0123456789

VENDETTA MEDIUM ITALIC

ABCDEFGHIJKLMNO
PQRSTUVWXYZ
abcdefghijklmnopqrstu
vwxyz0123456789

VENDETTA MEDIUM SMALL CAPS

ABCDEFGHIJKLMNOPQ
RSTUVWXYZ

Light 1234
Light Italic 1234
LIGHT SMALL CAPS 1234
LIGHT PETITE CAPS 1234
⅓ ⅝ ⅖ ¼ ✿ ❧ ❦ 1234
Bold 1234
$95

Medium 1234
Medium Italic 1234
MEDIUM SMALL CAPS 1234
MEDIUM PETITE CAPS 1234
⅓ ⅝ ⅖ ¼ ✿ ❧ ❦ 1234
Bold 1234
$95

Vendetta Volume: $179

———

John Downer is also responsible for the Emigre script logo, as well as the main type on the cover, Council, which was designed by him circa 1999. The graphic on the back cover is from Poppi, a picture font designed by Martin Friedl soon to be released by Emigre.

Emigre Product Info

Emigre Magazine

Emigre is published twice a year with issues coming out in February and August. As of February, 2004, *Emigre* has discontinued selling subscriptions, and will sell only single issues. All existing subscriptions will be honored.

Back Issues

Many back issues are available at the regular cover price. Collectors' issues (those which are available in very limited quantities) start at $25.

Emigre Fonts Catalog

To order a copy of the comprehensive Emigre Fonts Catalog go to:
www.emigre.com/EmigreCatalog.html

Books About Emigre

A number of books have been published about the work and history of Emigre; *Emigre (the Book): Graphic Design into the Digital Realm* (now in its 5th printing!), gives an overview of the founding of Emigre in 1984 and covers the first 10 years; *The Emigre Exhibition Catalog* was published as part of the Charles Nypels Award which Emigre won in 1996.

Emigre Music

Over the past 12 years Emigre Music has released 23 CDs, from Basehead's *Play With Toys* (voted by *Spin* magazine as one of the "90 Greatest Albums of the 90s"), to the recent inclusion of Scenic's latest CD, *The Acid Gospel Experience*, in *Emigre* #63. On our website you can download free MP3 samples of Emigre Music releases and read interviews with the musicians.

Miscellaneous

Emigre also offers T-shirts, artists' books, posters, wrapping paper, mousepads, and the always popular *Sampler Bag* containing a collection of Emigre goodies.

Mailing List

Help us keep our email and mailing lists up to date. You can change your email address, or take yourself off our mailing list at:
http://www.emigre.com/work/acct__login.php

All prices, shipping rates, schedules, and product availability are subject to change.

How to Order Emigre Fonts & Products

Order On-line

www.emigre.com

This is the most convenient way to order and you'll avoid font shipping costs. Fonts are available for immediate download, all other items are shipped within five business days.

Order by Fax

Print out a faxable order form at:

http://www.emigre.com/EFax.php

Fax: 530.756.1300

Order by Mail

Enclose payment by check or charge your credit card. All checks must be payable through a US bank, in US dollars.

Mail to:

Emigre
1700 Shattuck Ave., #307
Berkeley, CA 94709
USA

Emigre News

Add yourself to the Emigre News emailing list. We use Emigre News to help keep you informed of new products, services, and special limited offers.

To sign up go to:

www.emigre.com/enews

"The simple truth is that professional design will almost always fall short of touching hearts because it's second-hand love. Designers love doing design, the client is just a vehicle. Design is like a Cyrano de Bergerac who speaks irresistible words of love because of a passion for language. Roxane he can take or leave. If design loves anyone, it's Baron Christian."

— Kenneth FitzGerald, *I Come to Bury Graphic Design, Not to Praise It*, page 29.